TEXAS
A World in Itself

Books by
GEORGE SESSIONS PERRY

★

WALLS RISE UP, *a novel, Doubleday, Doran & Co.*

HOLD AUTUMN IN YOUR HAND, *a novel (National Book Award of* 1941),
The Viking Press.

THIRTY DAYS HATH SEPTEMBER, *a mystery, written in collaboration with
Dorothy Cameron Disney, Random House.*

TEXAS

A World in Itself

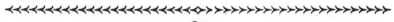

BY GEORGE SESSIONS PERRY

Illustrated by ARTHUR FULLER

Introduction by W. H. Cooke

PELICAN PUBLISHING COMPANY
GRETNA 1975

Manufactured in the United States of America

Published by Pelican Publishing Company, Inc.
630 Burmaster Street, Gretna, Louisiana 70053

If you ask why a man has run away from the States and come to Texas, "few persons feel insulted at such a question. They generally answer for some crime or other which they have committed; if they deny having committed any crime, or say they did not run away, they are generally looked upon rather suspiciously."

W. B. DEWEES
an early settler

Foreword

It is manifest that nobody is going to write all about Texas in any one book, or in any one reasonably long shelf of books. The subject is myriad, multifarious, and endless. Had I come down to Texas from the East, say, and made a six weeks' tour and then written a book, I might probably have done both a more cogent and a less prejudice-ridden job. That the book would have been superficial is another matter.

As it was, I'd spent a little better than thirty years collecting my material, and therefore had much too much of it. Tons of it had to be jettisoned, and among those tons will be what some readers may consider the most interesting subjects, particularly if those readers be collectors and experts on Texana.

There were many old-timers such as Big-Foot Wallace and Charles Goodnight who are worthy of space in anybody's book, but who could not be introduced into this one because its purpose was largely to depict, or at least give an impression of, the contemporary scene.

There was no room for the detailed lore of cattle, cotton, oil, and lumber. Great reservoirs of grand stuff that had to be left out. I should have liked, for example, to go into the way it feels to run the sucker at a gin in cotton picking time—of the feeling of power that comes to the operator as he plunges the ten-inch-wide sucker pipe into a wagon-load of cotton and makes it disappear as if by magic.

Nor was there space in which to tell how it feels to be a derrick man, working on a narrow thimble-board high in the top of a derrick at night—of the rumors that he hears—of the secrets he may keep or sell.

Nor was there room to elaborate on the blessedness of a south breeze on a summer night when you're sitting on a curb in a small Texas town, looking up at the warm clear stars while you are surrounded by darkened store buildings. Of the things that pass through your mind as you sit there, of what you are able to reconstruct by the passage of a few cars down the street. For by them you know who's sick, who's courting, who's drunk, who's talking to whom about what.

There was little space for dogs and coons, not half enough for all the old tales.

I should have liked to tell of the Galveston storm of 1900, perhaps the greatest natural disaster ever to hit Texas, killing several thousand people and demolishing the city. At the time, my father-in-law, Dr. O. S. Hodges, had just begun the practice of medicine there. Going from his office to the boardinghouse where he lived, he waded shoulder deep in water. Halfway home, a sailing roof tile cut the top out of his hat. When he reached the boardinghouse, he found it full of frightened

women. After the water of the tidal wave had risen to
the second story, one of the women suggested reading a
verse or two out of the Bible. Perhaps some message or
omen of hope would come to them. At random she
opened the Bible and began reading aloud. The verse
was: "In the midst of life, we are in death." She groaned
and closed the book.

Exigencies of organization prohibited the story of
Uncle Withy, an ancient Negro man who had worked for
the railroad all his life. One day a new division superintendent saw Uncle Withy tottering down the tracks and,
because of his advanced age, had him fired. Uncle Withy
wrote a letter to the president of the railroad: "I was
working on this road when you was a little boy. Now
some stranger come along and told me I was fired. You
kin fire me all you wants to, but I ain't gonna quit."
The president of the road, having no other alternative,
put Uncle Withy back on the payroll.

Later, on a pass, Uncle Withy took a trip to Los
Angeles. The news he brought back to us homefolks was
that the streets of that distant city were all named in
Latin and Greek, and the house numbers ran into the
"frillions."

Finally, I have said very little about how much horse
sense the ordinary Texan has. If you're all right,
Texans divine it and accept you, and unless you aren't
accepted you'll never know how much that means. If
you're not quite on the level, you'll just tread water in
Texas and never be standing on solid ground—and
money won't make the difference.

About seven years ago, Frank Rosengren and his wife hit San Antonio with very little money, a sick boy, and the intention of opening a book shop. The probability that the book shop would succeed was extremely slight. Yet for some mysterious reason, Frank felt immediately that he'd come not to a strange land, but home. He says he felt somehow kind of rested.

A week or so later on Christmas morning, when Frank went outside his door, he almost broke his neck he stumbled over so many Christmas presents. And for the rest of the day these theoretically lonely strangers hadn't a second to call their own —so many people were calling up to see if they wouldn't come over for a drink of whisky and a piece of fruit cake.

Now it doesn't take any especial powers of discernment to know that the Rosengrens are of the good people of this earth. But it does, I think, if you haven't even seen them. Anyway, that's what happened.

In the few years this Yankee family has lived in the somewhat tough and rusty and genuine old city of San Antonio, it's collected more real friends than it ever had anywhere else. And the Rosengrens don't belong to any clubs and people in San Antonio don't like books, which is what the Rosengrens are most interested in and, now and then, sell.

Moral: when you come to Texas, just be right inside and don't worry.

Texas is, and certainly isn't worrying.

GEORGE SESSIONS PERRY.

Introduction

W hen George Sessions Perry's *Texas: A World in Itself* was first published in 1942, it was recognized as one of the most unusual books about Texas ever published. After it went out of print, readers hoped that one day some publishing house would reissue this fresh approach by a brash young man who wrote about his native state. We have had to wait far too long, and this edition will be welcomed eagerly.

Perry's *Texas* has authenticity. There are some typical Texas brags included in the book, but the author also takes fun pokes at the natives that are a joy to both non-Texans and Texans. There are tales about the pompous and the rascals, intimate tales told with an impish wit. The book is filled with folklore and history; the chapter on the Battle of the Alamo makes the reader feel he is right at the side of Davy Crockett, Barrett Travis, Ben Milam, Jim Bowie, and the others. It is actual history written like fiction—and you are there.

A native of Rockdale, Texas, George bought a summer home in Connecticut in his more lucrative years when the rejection slips were replaced by healthy checks from publishers and magazines. Also about this time he purchased the farm near Rockdale that was the setting for *Hold Autumn in Your Hand*, which won the National Book Award for 1941.

George Sessions Perry was a typical big Texan, every inch of him filled with enthusiasm. He was meticulous in all his research; yet he threw himself into his writing full speed ahead and damn the details like periods and commas (Claire, his wife, would take care of those little things when she typed his manuscript).

Upon buying the Texas farm, George immediately picked up a telephone and called a close friend, Mike Lee, in Rockdale, telling him, "Have somebody build me a barn." Mike asked, "What kind of barn? How big?" But George couldn't be bothered with details: "A red barn." Period. With these simple instructions, he got his barn built. Mike, who knew about such things, threw in such specifications as size, cattle and horse accommodations, feed troughs, loft, and other odds and ends, just like Claire threw in the punctuation marks and corrections when she typed George's manuscripts. Mike says, "It was a dinger of a red barn!"

George scorned the typewriter, writing his stories in longhand, using a pencil and pencil tablet. His favorite writing position was lying on his stomach on the living-room floor with his two house-broken bird dogs flanking him in equally comfortable positions. They liked the nearness of their master and probably felt that they, too, had a part in what he was writing. Sometimes George flopped his big frame on a bed, rolled to one side, rested his head on one hand, and wrote furiously on his pencil tablet as the ideas flowed through his mind.

George Sessions Perry was born on May 5, 1910. Forty-six years later, on December 13, 1956, he disappeared in a river near his home in Guilford, Connecticut. Two months later, on

February 13, 1957, his body was recovered, and he was buried in his hometown of Rockdale on February 19.

George graduated from Rockdale High School in 1927. He met Claire Hodges of Beaumont while both were attending Southwestern University in Georgetown, Texas. They were married in 1933.

He admitted his enthusiasm for college never reached an all-time high, saying, "I never did get past my freshman year." Between attending Purdue University and the University of Houston, he made one trip to Europe as a deck boy on a freighter, and another trip on a passenger liner. On the latter trip he remained in North Africa six months, "just pleasantly spending the time."

When he was only eighteen years old, George made up his mind to be a writer. He tried doing a little newspaper writing with me for the weekly *Rockdale Reporter*. I remember when we both took a flight in a barnstorming old war biplane that was held together with assorted pieces of baling wire. The pilot had landed in a field near Rockdale and was giving rides at two dollars per person—two at a time crowded into an open cockpit. George wrote a little feature story about his first airplane ride. His fearful comment in the second paragraph was: "When I looked down as we passed over town, the first thing I saw was a cemetery."

Newspaper reporting, he decided, was not his bag. He then tried his hand at fiction and stuck with it through long years that were rewarded by rejection slips. He wrote half a dozen unpublished novels before he turned to the short story. He sold his first story to the *Saturday Evening Post* in 1937. After so many failures, the sale came as a shock to both George and Claire. In the ensuing years he took success in large doses, writing a dozen successful books in addition to more than a hundred magazine stories, fiction and nonfiction. During World War II he represented the *New Yorker* as correspondent in North Africa and the *Post* as a navy correspondent in the invasion of Sicily and Southern France.

Claire shared George's disappointments and his successes. Their relationship was so close that people who knew them best said, "George and Claire" almost as though they were talking about a single individual. Claire died in Guilford, Wednesday, February 12, 1975, almost nineteen years after George's death, and was buried by his side in a Rockdale cemetery February 19.

This reissue of *Texas: A World in Itself* comes when a new generation is ready to enjoy this "bodacious" tale about Texas. Moreover, appearing soon after the death of Claire, it is a timely memorial to the wife who helped her husband attain success as a writer.

W. H. Cooke, Publisher
The Rockdale Reporter
Rockdale, Texas

Contents

TEXAS
A World in Itself

1. How Texas Looked from a Distance

$\mathcal{E}$VERY year when I was a boy, my mother and I would leave Texas late in June and go to Indiana to visit my great-grandfather. The main reason for these trips, of course, was to avoid the blistering Texas summers. But the weather was not the only thing that was different and milder. The things in Indiana that always seemed least like home to me were the extremely small number of fist fights between the boys of my age, the almost heavenly luxury of going barefoot without having to beware of sand burs, and the fact that people expected me to eat rhubarb.

But the very temper of the land was different too. The Indiana land gave the feeling of having been tamed. It was a greener land, where the rains fell, so it seemed to me, almost as needed. It was a fat, almost a jolly, land. There was about it none of the quality of unbridled recalcitrance which emanated from the land at home.

The people seemed more cautious than Texans; the cities were dingier than ours. That the farmers might have such tidy, almost universally painted houses, such huge and well-kept barns, surpassed my understanding. The fine big barns I now understand: the colder climate necessitates them. But the neat, comfortable, even dignified farmhouses are still something of a mystery to me. In Texas we not only haven't got them, we never, within my memory, had them, except of course in rare cases.

Ten years or so after these Indiana visits began, I, as quite a young man, took a job in Chicago, selling lamp shades. Here I felt far more at home than I'd ever felt in Indiana. Chicago was brash and young and boasting and growing. Its people were greedy for fun and money. Here the cost of things was not much counted. If you wanted something, you set out to get it, and kept on trying until you did. Like Texas it was not especially civilized, but, also like Texas, it was intoxicated with its own vigor, amazed by its own growth and wealth and bulging muscles. Its philosophy, like that of Texas, was the philosophy of action, gain and growth.

And yet there were the gangsters. Capone ran the town. And the whole nation wondered why nobody did anything about it. Chicagoans knew, were in a minor way secretly proud, of the appalling graft that tied the hands of law enforcement agencies. If a citizen went into a night club and found the waiters mopping the floor, removing the signs of carnage where, a few moments earlier, a gangster had been liquidated by a competitor, he was not surprised. If after the day's work a commuter were riding home on the I. C. and the train stopped between stations, he knew the boys had stuck it up again, that somebody aboard was carrying a payroll that would never reach its destination. The killings rose from tens to scores, and still no hand was raised against the gangsters. And to me, a Texas boy, that was inconceivable.

Suppose the gangsters should have attempted to carry on similar activities in Houston or Dallas or San Antonio?

It would have been unwise. For while petty crooks may flourish in these towns year after year, they operate humbly in the shadows. If a Texan wishes to perpetrate business frauds, and if he pays off discreetly, he may succeed. There are also, of course, great opportunities in our state for political dishonesty. But if an indiscreet soul branches out into the realm of physical violence, as did the Chicago racketeers, it is not well for him to take up a permanent abode in Texas. For he will have planted a quivering ambition in the hearts of the Texas constabulary.

The city policemen may still be amenable to reason, may roll over accommodatingly, and play dead. But half of the country sheriffs will be hungry for the sight of him; so will two-thirds of the highway police, and all of the Texas Rangers. Their competitive spirit will have been aroused. His breach of the civil peace they will regard as an attack upon their dignity as the guardians of that peace. No longer are bribes acceptable. Their pride, their belief in the legend that they are the guttiest men on earth, has become involved. And with unerring certainty they'll cut him down.

It is true we've had our Sam Basses, our Clyde Barrows, our Bonnie Parkers. But these people kept moving. They did not, while monopolizing our front pages, set up stationary empires of crime and gun our people into submission, as was the case in Chicago. Our outlaw gunmen have all had the same history: they lived on the go and were killed on the wing.

From Chicago a number of pleasant miscalculations and accidents took me to Algeria in French North Africa.

I was there, among other seasons, in July and August, and found the climate quite similar to that in Central Texas. On those particularly uncomfortable summer days when the sirocco—a south wind from the Sahara—filled our houses and clothes with grains of hot sand, I was reminded of summer days in Texas when a burning wind bore ochre clouds of sand from the Dust Bowl while the temperature stood at a hundred degrees Fahrenheit.

Here in Algeria I found far greater race discrimination between the French and the Arabs than I had ever seen between the Texans and the Mexicans or Negroes in their midst. Not that the rich sheiks were not welcome in the hotels and cafes. It was the poor Arabs who were treated worse than animals. I saw them hitched to wagons and carts, dragging their terrific burdens up the steep hillsides. Their day's wage, the equivalent of an American five-cent piece, was less even than the Negroes and Mexicans were paid at home. For I had never known of their being paid less than fifty cents a day, so long as the worker furnished his own food and shelter.

However I did find among the Arabs the same love of pepper, of gaudy colors and ornaments, that exists among our Texas Mexicans. I also found in the Arabs the same readiness for personal violence, the same reluctance to engage in orderly group action that characterizes the Mexicans, and, to a large extent, the Texans. Finally, I found that all poor people, both in Texas and out, are usually constrained to cook their meals in one pot.

When I went from Algiers to France, the French seemed most like Texans in their determination not to be *made* to do anything. Their most divergent trait seemed to be a basic, almost Chinese, cynicism. The Texans like to believe, and they like to fight for what they believe. The French had the disillusionment that comes with wisdom or, at least, just before it.

From France I went to New York. Here more than anywhere else was Texas: raw wiry strength, youth, fantastic growth, spectacular height of skyscrapers substituting for spectacular breadth of land. Here, combed from the rest of the nation, as Texas had earlier combed them, were the adventurers, the daring thieves, the striving ones, the riskers, the majestic frauds.

I felt wonderfully at home. Sam Houston would have loved this town. It was big enough to take him. Its one deficiency from Sam's viewpoint would have been the lack of Indians—the people to whom he always returned for spiritual poise whenever conflict and the harassment of events had wrecked his own. On this teeming island there were no quiet places with walls thick enough for an outlander to cease to feel the exterior crush and the torrents of traffic kept flowing over streets, on elevated trestles, through subterranean tubes, at what oceanic expense of human energy; through the walls one could also sense the thousand skeins and webs of human conflict—millions struggling first for space, where there was not enough, and then for money and power and fame.

I loved this town with its hard and brutal glitter, its appalling provincialism, and its genuineness. But I also knew it was tougher than I was, or that, at least, my own defenses, conditioned by a Texas boyhood, were not somehow applicable. They would not be effective in the battle for existence in this tough and wonderful town. In Texas it seemed most of the men I'd known had staked out a claim on a dream of one kind or another. In pursuing it, their inflexibility of purpose would stand them in good stead even here—but not the inflexibility of means that seemed to be ours.

I felt that the New York politicos might out-maneuver Jim Ferguson, that the crowd would swallow up Amon

Carter and kill him with anonymity. I thought of certain of the most talented thieves among the new crop of Texas big shots. They were all good on their home grounds, but in New York they'd probably be taken.

But aside from the toughness and boasting of the Texan and the New Yorker, their dreaming and their strength, the ultimate similarity between them seemed to me the fact that either is always a prospect for what's known as "a bill of goods." In both places the open, the reachable, swayable mind predominates, and if you've got a scheme for doing or gaining something, you'll find people in either of those places who'll put in with you.

I went back home to the Indians for hurried repairs.

Then to Hollywood, where I saw the worst qualities we Texans possess carried to the point of absurdity. The touch of exhibitionism which in ourselves I'd always considered rather pleasant, a lively manifestation of our healthiness and youth, I found not only distastefully exaggerated there, but unrelieved by our staying power and our genuine if naïve beliefs.

From the celluloid city I went to the place which, more than all others, was least like Texas (I'm not forgetting France), and that place was New England.

One reason for this, I think, is the land. Connecticut's land is brutally poor and stony. Their winters would chill if not freeze the soul. The people who settled there had come a long way looking for the promised land— and this was the bitter substitute for fulfillment.

It would seem that those who were not broken by this experience would have moved on. Those who stayed are cautious, conservative people, and many, I fear, are a little sour. I do not, of course, refer to the latter-day Connecticut crowd, the retired New York brokers, the working artists with whom the place crawls, or the incredible hordes of Italian working people.

The Old Line Connecticut people could only, on close association with the Texans, regard them as a foolhardy, profligate, unreliable and impetuous people, who are, generally speaking, transients. I don't think the Connecticut people could honestly respect a group whose houses seldom last more than fifty years, and I don't imagine they would accept termites as a valid excuse.

For what they get, Connecticut people, aside from the unearned increment group, work harder than we do. This would be so even if their work were spread evenly over the entire year. Mostly, except in the factories, it isn't. Their season of good weather is short, and almost all outside work must be completed before it's over. Cattle and chickens must be kept in heated barns, while ours graze abroad and make their own livings. Many of us Texans could make the winter on what the Easterners pay for fuel.

Perhaps that has something to do with the apparent fact (and it may be more apparent than real) that Texans are slightly more generous. Because whatever a Texan gives you—an hour of his time, a baked sweet potato, a drink of whisky—it's probably cost him less labor and anguish of spirit than it would his countryman from the Northeast. In other words, when the Texan gives the same, he gives less.

But if Texas is least like New England, what is it most like? Oddly enough it reminds me most of a place I've never seen, and of which I may have an erroneous idea. And that is the home of the Aussies, Down Under.

Sam Houston and Barret Travis might well have been Aussies. So might Jim Ferguson or Coke Stevenson— even if the Aussies would probably have busted Lee O'Daniel's microphone. Strap Buckner and Praxiteles Swann, Roy Bean and Amon Carter—all of them might very well have been Aussies.

And then there is another one.

Perhaps in conveying the central feeling of anything so vast and various as Texas, it might be well to mention a man who has grown out of its soil and traditions, a man whose nature, however many-sided, could nevertheless symbolize and represent the character of his state. And to find such a man not much searching is required. At once Frank Dobie springs to mind. He's as unmistakably Texan as a Longhorn steer, as the sight of a lone cowboy laying his freshly fried bacon in neat strips on an absorbent plop of last year's cow dung to drain off the grease.

I have stood outside a western ranch house on a cold clear night, looking at the bright stars, seeing the silent land stretching forever away, knowing that out in the chaparral the buck deer was roving, that soon the frost would fall and the rattlesnakes grow still. The night was clean with the cleanness of alkali, a night so clean, so hard and bright, that to stand in it was almost a religious experience. And yet I was a stranger from the cotton fields of Central Texas. For me this night was a separate thing, not part of a long continuum, of a lifetime of such nights.

This was Frank Dobie's land. He has ridden it, lived it, loved and hated it into his blood—the breadth, the thorns, the vast clarity. On it he's ridden herd while his fellows slept, has watched the bedded cattle and, full of a quiet loneliness, a gentle, painless sadness, has sung to them. He has known all the depths and solitude of these nights, all of their edged beauty.

He knows this country better, I think, and by it has been more elevated, than any man who ever sweated the band out of a Stetson hat. He is rooted in this land not only by birth and affection. His intimately felt past goes beyond his birth, reaches out to the Rangers, the cow waddies, the great lead steers that paced the herds to Kansas City, to the outlaw horses and the outlaw men who roamed this hard land, who patched their harness and houses and lives with rawhide. And sometimes he is lonely for them.

During the winter he is a professor at the University of Texas, where he teaches young Texans about the Southwest. Most of what he teaches them, he dug out of the fading past himself. Many of the books on the Southwest, certainly some of the best of them, were written by him. He is an authority on lost mines and buried treasure within our sprawling neighborhood. He knows more about a coyote than its mother does. And I privately suspect that sometimes, at the end of the school year when he starts back to the ranch country, it is only with

the most violent restraint that he passes the first grazing
steer he sees without kissing it.

In looks, he resembles Carl Sandburg somewhat,
except Dobie's got more go. Already his hair is white.
But the light in his eye is the light of youth and humor.
Actually I think Dobie's greatest fear is that "the acade-
micians," as he usually refers to his colleagues at the
University, will one day, not by any compulsion but by
placid example, tame him and kill his spirit. But they
won't, nor will the years.

Frank Dobie is a gentle, modest, violent, generous man
who says no when he means no, and who, I suspect,
would not take one backward step before the devil carrying a bowie knife. Once in Austin he got a parking ticket
that he thought he didn't deserve. A two-dollar fine
would have satisfied the demands of the law. But Dobie
thought he was innocent and that to pay the fine would
compromise his integrity. He went to jail and "laid out"
his sentence. The University, meanwhile, had to wait.

I first met him on a wolf hunt in South Texas. He was
wearing some scuffed old high-heeled boots, about a
dollar and a half's worth of clothes, and a Stetson hat
that would keep the sun off his face. He was starved and
eating stew with both knife and fork as he listened to an
old rancher tell an old tale. I never saw a happier man.

Then when the hunt was over, three cowboys, one
with a fiddle, two with guitars, sang a song:

> Rye whisky, rye whisky,
> Rye whisky I cry,
> Rye whisky, rye whisky
> I'll drink till I die.

That was all the words said, but you could tell what a good time these cowboys had had, how lonesome they were before we came, how lonesome they were going to be after we left, how really terribly they hated to see us go.

It got me. Right in the throat. I knew my eyes were getting wet, and I was ashamed to be seen in this condition. I glanced around to see how Dobie was taking it. He had fled. To emote, I suppose, in private, as a Texan should.

A year or two later I was at Dobie's house one day and Mrs. Dobie mentioned that her husband had bought a few head of cattle and had had them put on a ranch to be looked after while he taught school. But she also mentioned that he had got a new branding iron.

I could visualize him there in Austin with this new, and to him, I felt sure, sacred instrument. Looking down at the floor he could imagine a thrown calf there, the pants stretched tight over a cowboy's knees holding the calf. Dobie could feel the heat from the wood fire, sense the jab of the hot iron, smell the strong stinking fumes of burnt hair and hide, and see the now-released, now-stinging calf, running away bucking and kicking.

But in that Austin living room there had been none of the Dobie cattle. So, Mrs. Dobie told me, he had gone outside and built himself a little fire and branded the garage door. On the inside.

While most of us contemporary inhabitants of the state are only Texans, Dobie, to the square toes of his high-heeled boots, is a Texian, as our forefathers of the Sam Houston vintage and voltage styled themselves.

Dobie would have been a good man at San Jacinto. He would have been just as good at the Alamo.

It is therefore, with great affection and respect, that I dedicate this book about Texas to the Texian who knows most about her and loves her best, my friend, Frank Dobie.

2. A Few Texas Firsts and Worsts

*I*T's extremely difficult to give a stranger a few casual and general notions about Texas without appearing to be either dangerously intemperate or a liar. It is so vast and spectacular that a really reasonable person can hardly afford to believe the truth. A few people have gone on record as not liking anything about it. General Sherman said that if he owned Texas and Hell, he'd rent out Texas and live in Hell. Well, if he'd rented it for as little as a dollar per square mile per year, the general probably could have managed to scrape by on his income—which would have been in excess of a quarter of a million dollars a year.

Yes, it's that big—too big, actually, to visualize in

one hunk. It's better to think of it, for the moment, as a group of federated realms, then turn to page 140 of our local Bible, *The Texas Almanac*, and read that: "Texas has in its pine timber belt an area as large as Indiana. Texas has an area along the coast, lying less than 150 feet above sea level and having a sub-tropical climate, equal to the area of South Carolina. Texas has an area lying in a middle temperature climate and ranging from 3,000 to 4,000 feet above sea level . . . as large as Pennsylvania. Texas has a mountainous area west of the Pecos as large as West Virginia. Texas has a uniformly good farming country, well watered and ranging in altitude from 200 to 2,500 feet above sea level, situated in central and mid-west parts of the state, equal to the areas of Ohio and Kentucky. Texas has an area on the Edwards Plateau, admirably adapted to cattle, sheep and goat raising and diversified crop production, as large as Tennessee." Its maximum length is 801 miles, its breadth, 773.

As a matter of fact, when Texas joined the union in 1845, she reserved the right to subdivide at her discretion into five sovereign states. But Texas, at that point, was very much like the young Tennesseean who, during the Texas-Mexico War in 1836, was packing his gear and getting ready to leave home. When asked what was up, he said, "I'm going to Texas to fight for my rights."

Well Texas got her rights, but she'll never exercise them. As Frank Dobie says, "If you split up the state, who'd get the Alamo?"

Now nobody will tell you quicker about his own state's less rosy aspects than a Texan, though of course he'd probably have a fist fight with a non-Texan for putting it half so strongly.

The Texan will tell you that in West Texas you have to dig for wood (grub mesquite roots) and climb (canyons) for water.

On the walls of a West Texas dug-out one discouraged soul wrote:

> 20 miles to water.
> 10 miles to wood.
> 6 inches to Hell.
> > Gone Back East to Wife's Family.
> > Make Yourself at Home.

Hear one of the many stanzas of "Hell in Texas":

> The devil was given permission one day
> To make him a land for his own special sway.
> He scattered tarantulas over the roads.
> Put thorns on the cactus and horns on the toads;
> He lengthened the horns of the Texas steer
> And added a foot to the jack rabbit's ear.
> He hung thorns and brambles on all the trees,
> He mixed up the dust with a million fleas.
> He quickened the buck of the bronco steed,
> And poisoned the feet of the centipede.
> The heat in the summer's a hundred and ten,
> Too hot for the Devil and too hot for men.

In West Texas people boast about the wind and sand storms. When asked if the wind blows that way the year around, they're apt to reply, "No, a big part of the time it blows the other way."

Again, a Texan may tell you that his is the state where there're more cows and less milk, more pasture and less grass, than anywhere else on earth. He may also mention that you can look farther and see less.

But a Texan knows that the fact that he is a Texan makes him "somebody." In Mexico a Texan carries more weight than a plain garden variety of *Americano*. The Texan knows that the run of people in the United States are more interested in his state than most others, which he considers perfectly natural, and that they expect him to be a person of unusual interest. He has, in fact, to be a little careful not to fall into the manner of a combination train robber and rodeo hand—in a simple desire to keep people from being disappointed. Especially do little boys have this trouble. I recall the staggering lies I told the Indiana small fry when I visited my grandfather there. As a matter of fact, I was raised more or less in the saddle, yet I really hadn't killed any Indians or twelve-foot rattlesnakes. But like most people, those Indiana boys asked for it with their leaping credulity.

The fact that Texans vary widely, that a Houston banker may have more in common with the Wall Street broker than with the Brush Country rancher, never enters most people's minds; nor that much of the border country's political machinery is more Mexican in its general characteristics than American; nor that many East Texas Piney Woods localities smack more of Mississippi than of Texas, and that the rice section around Beaumont is very Louisiana.

Many of these divergencies are due to the state's appalling size, and the overlapping influence of its neighbors. But the most basic reason is the character of

Texas' annual rainfall, which in general decreases five inches per hundred miles as one travels inland from the Gulf. For a majority of Texans earn their livelihood from varying combinations of earth and work and weather. And our ways of earning a living naturally have a great influence in making us what we are.

To give you a notion of what those earning patterns are, let me, for a moment, pummel you with a few huge facts. You already know that Texas produces more cotton than any state in the union. The same is true of beef, grain sorghum, sheep and goats. We produce forty per cent of the nation's oil, eighty-five per cent of its mined sulphur. Too, there are mountains of pine lumber, oceans of tomatoes, lettuce, grapefruit. Crystal City, deep in the Brush Country, calls itself "the Spinach Capital of the World," and its patron is Saint Popeye, *marinarius*. In the Texas Panhandle is the world's largest wheat field.

And very much to the point is the fact that Texans aren't producing these floods of commodities for love. Many of them are getting rich.

When the depression came along, Texas scudded through it with all flags flying. Texas payrolls dropped only five per cent, while those of the nation plunged twenty-seven per cent. At the same time, Texas was opening three hundred new plants, and moving from twenty-sixth to twelfth place among manufacturing states, with a billion-and-a-half-dollar output.

True, our luck was prodigious, and oil was drenching the land. The University of Texas had collected twenty-two million dollars in oil royalties from its West Texas holdings. And Victor Borsodi, flat broke in Houston, was serenely refusing a quarter of a million dollars for twenty acres of land because he felt the bid was too low.

Yet at the same time the cotton farmers, except those who had profited from oil leases, were going further in the hole all the time. And though Texans are at least adequately bull-headed, the farmers began to let that hot potato drop. For, in a degree not comparable to the Old South, Texans learn. And at least in the realm of economics, having learned, they mend their ways.

In their traditions, however, no fickleness is manifest. Whatever a man's code of ethics may be, if he is one of those rare thieves who believe in honor among their kind, and by them his character is described as "old Texas," that means something.

We Texans have a short past—it extends over about a hundred years in time, but it has been a turbulent, rip-snorting, hell-for-leather past, and it has made a deep impress on our lives and ways.

But before exploring that past, it might be well to isolate and look at the great hunks of land, the vast sections that together fill out the face of Texas.

3. Where Louisiana Leaves Off

*J*F A traveler entering Texas on his way from New Orleans to Houston were not informed of this momentous fact, he would in all likelihood think nothing had happened. Though he was across the state line at its southeasternmost part and had entered Texas' coastal prairies, he would still be in a semi-tropical land dominated, Louisiana style, by big rains, big landowners, and big mosquitoes. He'd still hear French spoken, still be in a flat land where bayous wind their sluggish ways over the marshy prairies and through the cypress swamps. The pinelands, whose principal yield is, of course, lumber and poor folk, lies to the northward.

The traveler would doubtless have crossed the line at the town of Orange. Here Lutcher Stark, a kind of philanthropic Caesar, with a finger in every pie, is the big noise. Thirty miles farther inland lies Beaumont, a rice and oil refining town, and ninety miles farther west is Houston. In this tiny corner of Texas nestles more than a third of America's oil refining capacity.

These refineries are owned by certain *nouveau riche* Eastern families like the Rockefellers and the Mellons. The remainder of this section, the land and the fruit of the land, belongs chiefly to the Starks, the Broussards, the Moodys, the Kirbys, the Boyts, and associated suzerains of old Texas stock. The warm tropical climate seems peculiarly suited to that species of fauna known as the land baron or, if you want to be rude, *terra porcus*.

Not of course that there are not divers and entrancing ways here of earning a living without either land or capital. One friend of mine, a man of great spiritual poise and contentment, lives by dragging cypress logs out of the swamps, splitting the cypress hearts into "fence posties" and selling them. And the fact that such logs are growing "skase" does not shatter his inner serenity. He's got a few rowboats which he rents for twenty-five cents an afternoon to such fishermen as apply for them. "We'll make out," he says with calm belief (the "we" referring to the wife that lives with him in the old jacked-up houseboat). "Heap o' times befo'," he points out, "we been whettin' on the point, but we always skunt through somehow."

And of course he will, because the swamps offer many ways to earn a living. The moss gin, where Spanish moss is ginned and combed like cotton, will pay forty cents a hundred pounds for as much dry moss as your boat will carry—and every swamp tree is loaded with it. Besides, bayou catfish bring a decent price; so do coon hides, and muskrat, which abound in the marshes. Finally, there's always bootlegging, which the heavy federal tax on legally distilled whisky is bringing back into vogue. The current price of moonshine whisky in this section now stands at about two-fifty a gallon against a minimum of ten dollars a gallon for the non-contraband.

But if these pursuits are found to be either too strenuous or risky, it is but a short distance to the Gulf coast where a man can exist by beachcombing and living on scrap fish such as mullet and croaker, which the commercial fishermen give away since their market value is nil. For the more energetic there are jobs with the shrimp fleet out of Galveston, or the snapper fleet which operates ninety miles out into the Gulf, and on which a man may earn for his share as high as twenty dollars a week. But this presupposes a heavy catch and a sore back, from hauling hour after hour on the tugging, hundred-foot lines.

Too, there is stevedoring, and there are refinery jobs, but these last are for people who stay put. The best thing, of course, is to have inherited a little empire of land all your own and to have the energy and ingenuity to make it pay. Some of the latter-day land barons of this section are not so gifted. Until now, however, petroleum and the whims of muskrats (muskrats are enormously valuable and trapping is done on shares) have kept them in clover.

Others, whom prosperity has not made soft and whom fate did not make simple, are making their realms bear fruit. And these are the Texans important to the future. Such a one is Pat Boyt, heir-apparent to the Boyt interests in Chambers and Liberty counties, a Texan to the core, and born, beyond any reasonable doubt, with a cocklebur under his tail.

Pat's granddaddy used to be a cattle drover, but his father got interested in rice, so they blended these two items, cattle and rice, into an economic scheme that appears to the observer an absolute cinch. Though the Boyts own only about 25,000 acres of land, they control through renewable leases some 90,000 acres in all. It's flat land, almost impossible to drain; the yearly rainfall is about four feet. Left to its owners, the land would have been almost worthless, because a marsh pasture is the rough equivalent of none at all.

Into this vast 90,000-acre loblolly, the Boyts cut forty-five miles of main canal, two hundred miles of lateral canals. These ran along the slight ridges so that water would flow out of them into the prospective rice fields. But that was only half the job. Just as much earthwork was necessary to build another set of canals for drainage.

This done, they built a pumping station on the Trinity River which would raise enough water to irrigate 25,000 acres of rice. It was not necessary to flood more than that much at a time because rice land must be allowed to lie idle at least two years out of three. And the years when the land is not in rice, it serves as abundant pasture for the 6,000 Boyt cattle.

By this arrangement the Boyts make money coming and going—the cattle living on the otherwise valueless by-product of the rice lands, land on which taxes would have to be paid anyhow. That, roughly, is the Boyt setup.

Driving out to meet Pat Boyt at the ranch house (only the foreman and the cow hands live there), I looked about me at the flat, too-well-watered land, smothered in its luxuriant growth of coarse, non-nutritious grasses. In many of the fields where rice had grown this year, the wet shocks still stood in the boggy fields. Men with what is known as butt-cutters were severing the less soggy tops of the rice shocks from their bottoms and threshing out the damp grain. Everywhere equipment was mired down. The sight of a tractor getting stuck while trying to pull an empty wagon was not unusual. Even now, when no rain fell, the air was damp and salty. Mosquitoes traveled in clouds. Why anybody would try to live in this disagreeable and depressing country was beyond me.

As I drove into Cottonwood, the headquarters of the Boyt ranch, I found myself in a sort of a compound of fifteen or twenty acres surrounded by corrals, Negro houses, bunkhouses, butcher houses, and stables. A little distance away was a metal barn that would house six hundred head of cattle.

I knew Cap Boyt, the ruler of the Boyt empire, was ill, and that Pat, the crown prince, was running the show.

I found Pat Boyt on the gallery of the H-shaped ranch house. He was reading a copy of *Time* and jumped as I came up on the porch. The engines of energy and tension inside him had started churning with a lurch.

At once he began telling me about an obstinate young tenant who was driving him crazy. This tenant was being so careful not to be a bootlicker that he wouldn't do anything he was told.

"Why don't you throw him off the place?" I asked.

"Because he's old Ned's boy," Boyt said. "Ned's been here thirty years." Abruptly he said, "What do you want to learn from me?"

"Something about East Texas cattle."

"Well most of the old-time tales you'd have to get from my father."

"That's not what I want," I said. "What's doing in East Texas ranching now?"

"So you think because I'm a young buck, I'll know more about that?"

There was a trace of belligerence in his voice.

"I can get the other stuff out of books," I said. "Besides, I just don't want it."

He went to work, talking fast and clearly, first voicing his annoyance at Texans in general for thinking of West Texas as "the cattle country," when there never was a time when there weren't more cattle per square mile in East Texas. Why? "Because we've always had more grass. You've got to have a little rain to have grass."

"What about the quality of the grass?" I was on the verge of saying, but I knew the West Texas grass was better. For fear of getting thrown out of the ranch house I desisted.

"There used to be an old Texas saying," he said, growing a little more calm, and answering my unasked question, "which said: 'Never take a cow east.' That was because a West Texas cow raised on richer grass hadn't a big enough belly to hold enough East Texas grass to live on. That's why our Longhorns were all belly. But we're improving the range by draining it and giving the native grasses a chance to contain something besides water. As the grass improves, we're improving the cattle.

"We started our up-breeding with Brahmas. We had lots of fever ticks then, and the Brahmas were more tick resistant. But the big freezes we had every ten years or so killed the Brahmas like flies. They haven't got any hair on their hides to speak of. But as we began to get rid of the fever ticks, we began to breed Hereford blood into our herds. Herefords have thick hair, and are of course better beef cattle. They've got their meat in the right places—where the expensive cuts come from. So now we've got a better beef strain, and a more freeze-resistant strain."

I said I'd always associated East Texas with scrub cattle.

"Look pardner," Boyt said, "this is America. People learn things here. Whatever they're doing, they do better every year."

Every statement he made was like a sentence out of a manifesto. Bristling.

"Another thing," he added as an afterthought to his discourse on herd improvement. "Herefords are calm.

With them we're breeding some of that Brahma wildness out of the cattle."

A Brahma, I well knew, was a wild and treacherous animal, docile one second, stampeding the next. Where most cattle only stampeded in large numbers, activated by the vagaries of crowd psychology, a Brahma was always capable of a solo stampede.

Boyt mentioned one instance where he had forty Brahma heifers penned with their calves. Out of a kind of roving restlessness the cows had trampled most of the calves to death.

"However," he pointed out, "given half of a chance, a Brahma calf, for the first six or eight months, will grow faster than any other animal on earth." And the preference of this nation for baby-beef gives that fact considerable meaning.

A moment later he was off on another tack. Incomprehensibly, to me at least, he said, "I love this land." For some minutes while I sat in amazement, he emphasized that statement. "It's the only place in America," he said "where cattle can make their own living without being fed at any time of any year."

I asked about the quality of the beef compared to that of West Texas. He said he thought the East Texas beef was just as good.

I don't. And the difference is a fundamental one that derives from the mineral content of the soil. For example, if you put one of a pair of twin calves in an East Texas pasture and gave it not only grass in abundance, but also as much East Texas corn as it would eat, its strictly range-fattened brother in West Texas would out-grow and out-develop it in every way.

"Maybe you think I've been trying to sell you East Texas," Boyt said. "Well now I'm going to tell you what's wrong with it."

In his bill of particulars, climate led all the rest. "It's unhealthy," he said, "mighty hard on both men and animals. Too damp. Sometimes the washing hangs on the line for three weeks without getting dry. Just mildews and ruins before you can take it down. That's one reason you see so many scrub horses here. Breed the mustang out of them and they can't stand the climate, and we never have been able to keep a breeding jackass over a year and a half. We give 'em the best of care, but the climate lays 'em low."

"What about the mosquitoes?" I asked. "Are they an economic factor in the cattle business? Do they make the cattle lose weight or are they just a nuisance to the cattle themselves?"

"A definite economic factor," he said. "They follow the cattle in clouds and sometimes walk them to death. Some of the calves they kill directly by sucking all their blood out."

Though a number of phone calls had come in for him, different men in his organization wanting to see him, he insisted on taking me to see the three breeding stallions which sired the ranch cow horses; all three of them were magnificent, short-coupled, quarter-mile racers from Kentucky.

The whole time we were looking at them, the feeder,

a sepia-skinned Negro, was stunting in the ranch yard with a trick mule, trying to catch our attention. Finally we pointedly watched him for a few minutes and made him terribly happy.

But now my host simply had to go. And yet, as we parted, he was unsatisfied with my visit. He had not had a chance to show me his most prized possession. This fast-talking, fast-thinking Texan, who had treated me with a peculiar mingling of helpfulness and defiance, this hard-fisted, intelligent man with an almost messianic belief in his own convictions, had not had time to show me his first love, the thing nearest his heart: his flower garden.

That was at his home fifteen miles away.

4. Cotton Folks

1

ROCKDALE, my home town, is Texas' heart and a significant part of its soul. Its story is more or less that of most Central Texas towns and of post-Civil War Texas, because it came into existence a good many years after Sam Houston *et al.* "hard-traded" the United States and joined it largely on Texas' own terms. Not long after that event, Texas lost its head and joined the Confederate rebellion, despite anything Sam Houston could do to stop it. Then, after the South's "moral victory" at Appomattox, many Southerners from "the Old States" were so hard up that they felt any change would be for the better. This restless element hitched up its wagons and came on to Texas.

The little group that landed at Rockdale selected this spot because the land was sandy. It was easy for a tired man and small, tired mules to plow. There were plenty of building posts at hand, and the land would grow the broad variety of items a pioneer family needed.

Only three or four miles to the north was the heavy, spectacularly fertile, black land, but the Rockdale folk were too tired, after their long, hard journey, to tackle it Besides, for the first few years, no land would grow much more cotton than the newly cleared sandy land.

The first big excitement after the little community was formed was the periodic visits of a gentleman from Indiana by the name of Samuel Bass, the celebrated train robber. He didn't rob any trains in Rockdale, but the only reason was that there weren't any. As a matter of fact, reports on Sam's actions in the "Regal City," as our weekly paper calls Rockdale, were never really carefully detailed, since our ladies were at home under the beds, and our downtown commercial personnel were under their counters.

Soon, however, there were rumors that the town might have some trains for Sam to rob, and this made many of our leading citizens furious. We were, they said, doing all right as we were, and let's not monkey with the *status quo*.

But the railroad came anyway, and, to the astonishment of its local opponents, the town boomed magically, particularly in the sublime period when Rockdale was the end of the line.

One of the most blessed aspects of the coming of the railroad was that it gave our people something to do. On Sunday afternoons, in particular, the arrival of the train was an important social event. Our ladies in their Sunday dresses, our gents in their blue serge suits, climbed into their buggies and went to the depot, there to fraternize and titter and show themselves off until such time as the iron horse should toot its whistle announcing its impending arrival.

Its arrival, however, was not the climax. That came when the engine crept out onto the turntable, and six men (ordinary mortals, mind you) pushed the thing bodily around so that it was heading in the right direction for its return trip.

This done, the train would soon depart for its destination at the other end of the line, and its admirers for their houses and the cold fried chicken that awaited them there.

Rockdale became a jovially prosperous, bustling, even exciting port of entry for all the world's goods, and people from the whole countryside came there to buy them.

There were two large wagon yards which each night were crowded with sleeping families—sleeping in the wagon beds if the night were fine, breathing in the exotic town air tinctured with wood smoke and cooking odors and cheap perfume, lulled by the musical, brittle crunch of horses eating corn out of feed bags. If the night were rainy, the families slept on the ground sheltered by the wagon beds.

Next day then, the trading and visiting re-began. Most prices were stable and non-confusing. A hen was worth a quarter, a turkey fifty cents. Eggs were a dime a dozen. Whisky was a nickel a drink or fifty cents a quart.

"The store" (as Scarbrough and Hicks in its eminence came to be called, while the other stores had to be designated by name) bought everything—calico, flour, bacon, salt, molasses, lard—in freight car lots and sold it on credit. If a man were short of cash, the store would lend him some and put it on the books. If he had too much cash on hand, he banked it at the store.

In a word, as an extremely benevolent boss, Mr. Hicks ran the town. But if Mr. Hicks was our commercial suzerain, Mrs. Hicks was the town's first lady, social arbiter, and senior member of a regency which built, directed, and controlled Rockdale's imposing stucco Baptist church. The other member of this regency was God.

Automatically, of course, Mrs. Hicks's house and her church across the street became the center of local social gravity, and, as the town grew, the merchant class all built their houses as near as possible to Mrs. Hicks.

In that way our town came to crystallize into districts of varying social importance. The section occupied by Mrs. Hicks and her satellites became known as Puddin' Ridge, the region across Ham Branch as Scuffle Gut, the very poorest white section being of course the Cabbage Patch, and the Negro section, Grassburr Hill.

At this time the great political battle over the destiny of "old Pied" was being fought out. The warring parties were the Wool Hat Gang on one side, and on the other the legions that followed Mrs. Hicks's snowy banner.

The Wool Hat Gang was categorically and violently opposed to uplift, the rich, and progress, in any of their manifestations. The loyalties of their opponents were just the opposite.

"Old Pied" was the stump-speaker's name for the family milk cow. The question had been whether old Pied should or should not be allowed to disport herself without let or hindrance on the town streets.

On the face of it, that would seem a mild and trivial issue indeed, which is precisely what it was not. Almost everybody in town had a close personal interest in the outcome.

In those days there was no such thing as a dairy, and most of the poorer citizens kept a milk cow. In this way not only was the family supplied with dairy products, but a little change could be garnered from the sale of extra butter and milk. And it was upon this surplus that the gentry depended, since most of the merchant class folk felt that it was not only too much trouble but a little beneath their station to tend and be encumbered with kine. On the other hand, they felt that flowers and pretty lawns were commensurate with their particular state of grace. Yet each time they attempted to grow flower gardens, these civic ornaments were casually devoured by some passing bossy. Moreover, the social upper crust regarded it a nuisance and an indignity to have to step off the plank sidewalks downtown to keep from falling over a recumbent cow, or perhaps being charged and gored by her boy friend. Finally, there was the question, and you may be sure it was an annoying one, of the untidiness that a healthy cow is prone to leave in her wake.

Yet the proposition that a milk cow's place is in the barn, and not on the *rues* and boulevards, was one of the most frequently defeated measures ever to come before the town. The issue resolved itself into a question of who should be made to build fences—the affluent to shut old Pied out, or the poor to keep her in—and every politician was forced to take sides on the issue.

There were certain of the more gifted demagogues that could fairly break their audience's hearts while pleading the cause of old Pied. The cow was, they said, not only man's best friend, but his greatest insurance against want. For when the cold-hearted flower growers and lenders of money turned their backs on you, old Pied would not discontinue her life-giving flow. All she asked for herself was a few wisps of grass from the side of the street. And yet those fiends, "the Old Respectables" (as the anti-Pied people were derisively called), wished to deny her this humble and God-given right. Apparently, it was pointed out, their secret, diabolical purpose was to scrape the butter off the bread of the poor.

Yet if some farmer who'd stayed in town to hear the speech started back to his wagon with a heart full of love for old Pied and found some passing heifer with her front knees in his wagon bed polishing off the last of his

sack of flour, he was apt to re-assess his political convictions and start beating her over the head with a hame.

Ultimately old Pied's cause, after many contests, was
lost so far as Rockdale was concerned. Yet over the
state at large, though motorists continue to kill themselves by colliding with cattle on the roads at night, old
Pied still holds sway—for the democratic reason that a
majority of Texans still want her to be free, and because
they know that for some reason the best grass grows at
the edge of the road.

By the time I was born, the store was a grand affair
with three departments: gent's furnishings, dry goods
and ladies' ready to wear, and a grocery with long
wooden counters and goods piled to the ceiling, per-
fumed by big simple smells, like those emanating from
five hundred pounds of onions, a ton of smoked bacon,
the astringent odor of case upon case of yellow lye soap,
and the gentle over-all smell of red, cranny-filling floor
sweep.

However it had passed its revenue-bearing prime and
was trying, with more or less success, to hold its own.
Not only was the land to the south exhausted, but the
influx of railroads to the surrounding towns had shrunk
its trade territory enormously. Also, Mr. Hicks had died,
and the Scarbroughs had withdrawn from the company
and gone to Austin to establish what was soon to become
one of the greatest mercantile businesses in the state.

With old Pied's defeat, uplift seemed to have got control of things in Rockdale. The citizens voted out the
pool halls, and finally, after we children of that time had

sung enough songs and carried enough heavy banners in parades down the main street, the saloons went too. After that blow, Rockdale became almost unbearably virtuous. No longer were we regaled by the impressive number of fist fights and knife duels to which we were accustomed, and upon which we'd somehow become emotionally dependent.

No longer were pleasant incidents like the following so likely to happen. One Christmas Eve a number of the local bloods were in one of the saloons conditioning themselves for the holidays, when a dirty, ragged young man came in to mooch a drink. By now most of the boys were full enough to want to do not just something, but something heroic. After standing the tramp to a couple of double whiskies, they took him out to a near-by pond and there stripped and scrubbed him. While this delousing was in progress, the committee on procurement was at Scarbrough and Hicks buying the best outfit of clothes in the house. When the now-sanitary tramp was diked out in this finery, the boys took him to town and bought him a turkey dinner. At its conclusion they stuck a ten-dollar bill in his pocket, bought him a ticket to a near-by town, and put him on the train. Now these rough-and-ready, well-intoxicated philanthropists dispersed to enjoy the holidays.

The young tramp, however, had got an enormous lift out of all this foolishness. When he left the train at the neighboring town, he was still full of turkey and high ambition. In a few hours he'd got a job. Today he is the leading merchant in that town.

In those old saloon days Rockdale was knowing its second boom. At that time it was shipping more lignite coal than any other spot on earth. The coal was mined by Mexicans who lived in huts about the mines and spent their pay in Rockdale. An old hunting friend of mine, then a youngster, borrowed fifteen hundred dollars on a ninety-day note and opened up a saloon. He hired a Mexican bartender and went after the Mexican trade. At the end of the ninety days he paid back the fifteen hundred and had twelve hundred dollars profit in the bank.

Then oil began to capture the lignite markets and Rockdale was slowly going broke. The yearly celebrations of *Cinco de Mayo* (Mexican Independence Day) out at the mines grew less exciting and colorful and bloody. Finally the mines closed entirely and the Mexicans drifted away.

And Rockdale, which, like Edna St. Vincent Millay, had built upon the sand, found its fields exhausted, and its one mineral gift without takers.

Then there came a torrential rain. In a day and a night it rained twenty-three inches—many times more than any living men could remember, and the flooding rivers drowned ninety of our people, leaving horrid mementoes, dead mules and bales of cotton, in the highest pecan and cottonwood trees. And then there came two years of burning, hopeless drouth and Rockdale was almost beaten when it received what might be called "the Texas salvation."

Oil was discovered just to the north of town—nothing spectacular, mind you, only a shallow field in which the wells averaged ten barrels a day, but they were cheap to dig and were dug by the hundreds, so that Rockdale was once more, if not booming, at least making expenses.

Again the evil day was postponed in which the people would have to face the fact that the land was empty of fertility and would grow no more cotton. For fifteen years the oil kept us going, but finally we had to make the adjustment, to abandon the ways and rhythms of our fathers who lived by cotton and corn alone.

Slowly then, as will be shown later, we began to learn that the connection of the turkey with Thanksgiving could have more than a gustatory connotation. We also began to turn cattle onto the resting land from which cotton had earlier driven them.

Now the thing that keeps us going week after week is the two thousand dollars' worth of eggs we sell between each Saturday and the next.

In this connection, there is the story of the hapless farmer who came into the hardware store one day and met his wife. The clerk was explaining to her the merits of a certain churn, but soon after the husband arrived, the clerk noticed the woman's attention wandering, saw her gaze focus on a small red stain on the man's lip. Now the woman's rage burst out. She grabbed the man's arm and shook him. "So you was getting that truck bed fixed!" she announced in loud sarcastic tones. "Oh no you weren't, Ace Huggins. Look at that red stuff on your mouth." Then with supreme anger she shook her finger in his face and said, "What you been doin' is spendin' my egg money for chile!"

"Egg money" has ceased to be a trivial source of farm income at Rockdale.

In many ways, then, the sons of the settlers of the sand are but just now accommodating themselves to the realities of their environment.

But with these changes much that was good is no longer with us. One night, three or four years ago, almost immediately after falling asleep I was waked by the town's fire siren. From my sleeping porch window I saw a blaze downtown and paused long enough in dressing to ask the telephone operator where the fire was. She said it was at the store—Scarbrough and Hicks.

That hit me like a dumdum bullet. It meant that something I had always assumed to be eternal, a part of the earth, and the bulwark of our town, was in peril.

Had it been my own house, which was insured and could have been rebuilt, I would have been less moved. The store, with which I had no financial connection, was a mere commercial enterprise, and yet I kept realizing that for forty years it had been a guarantee to our people against starvation. Here during the drouths and floods it had persevered. And when our people had come there, they had not had to have money, only a willingness to work, and they had been fed on trust. The store had been Rockdale's backbone and its splendor. But for the last fifteen years it had lived on borrowed time and money. If this fire destroyed it, it would, I knew, never be rebuilt.

Though the fire company from the adjoining town came to help our own, it was no use. When morning came, there was only a hideous scar where Scarbrough and Hicks had been. Now, even the tombstone of Rockdale's glory had been destroyed.

Like most little Texas towns, Rockdale is a cheap place to live, a hard place to earn much money. Perhaps the highest salary in the town is three hundred and seventy-five dollars a month, and it is unique. One or two persons may earn two hundred, a few a hundred and fifty, but most store managers and the like will probably average no more than a hundred. The clerks get about twelve dollars a week, and besides a few truck-driving jobs, the town offers little other business opportunity for a man without means.

One or two colored gardeners get as much as a dollar and a half for an eight-hour day. Most colored workers, however, get a straight dollar a day, the Wage and Hour Law notwithstanding. Their wives usually get a dollar a week for doing the laundry for a medium-sized family. And there are more colored women cooks in Rockdale who get two dollars and a half a week than there are those who get more. For most of the Negroes, cotton picking is the one bright spot in their economic scheme. Cotton picking is piecework, and the better pickers may sometimes earn several dollars a day.

War, of course, causes fluctuations in our pattern of wages and salaries and general income, but only temporary ones.

There are many farmers in the sand south of town who rarely earn as much as two hundred and fifty dol-

lars a year in cash. And, in the machine age, it is more
difficult for a man to "live at home" and exist in the
same century as his neighbors than it was a hundred
years ago when a cow and calf were legal tender representing a ten-dollar bill, and hogs and chickens were
change.

Nevertheless, when the cotton starts into town the
gins start running; the stores start selling. The bank's
small lobby is full of farmers. Some haven't had such
good luck. They are waiting now to plead for an extension of the mortgage on their mules and sparse, dilapi-
dated farm tools, to try to get another chance.

You can tell which are able to pay and which expect
to plead just by looking at their faces. You drop your
eyes and look away. You realize there is such a thing
as luck, and that it can be brutal. Sometimes you may
wonder how far back their bad luck started.

But the post office too does a thriving business now.
The outgoing mail to Sears, Roebuck is astonishingly
heavy, the in-rush of packages is commensurate; colored
ginghams, wool coats, single-shot .22's, cowboy boots, a
washpan, a bright oak dresser, a roll of roofing for that
place by the chimney where the shingles blew away.

Many half-pint customers at the liquor store become
pint and quart buyers. The incidence of Saturday night
street fights on Rat Row increases. Not until the early
hours of Sunday morning does the backfiring of Model
T's, Model A's, and old Chevvys cease to lambaste the
stillness of the night.

But even after the last celebrant has eaten the last

hamburger (and unless wind has dispelled it, the very pavement of Rat Row is pungent on Saturday night with the fat aroma of fried onions), when the last bottle has been emptied, and the man who runs the liquor store has refused to get out of bed to make one more sale, the trucks, the long trailer trucks loaded high with baled cotton, continue to roll through the town on their way to Houston.

Now another cotton crop is under our belt, the big thing, the central thing, has gone through another cycle. From it once more we may have failed to profit. But even so, there is a sideline that will cushion our disappointment. Soon the turkey market will open. In all probability the turkey crop hasn't been mortgaged, and is the bright spot in a generally dour picture.

2

It's November in the post-oak lands and the farmers are being noticeably polite to their wives, taking them not quite so for granted as they have through the summer and fall. Because the Thanksgiving turkey market has opened above fifteen cents, moving from sixteen to eighteen and back again. And while the farm women may consult their husbands on which day and to which buyer they should sell, the turkeys belong to the women, and it's in the turkeys, even more than in the five or six head of cattle that the farmer has raised, that the real money from this year's farm operation will come. It started as a tiny sideline to the main business of raising cotton, but on most of the sterile sandy-land farms, the turkey has long since supplanted cotton as the main source of income.

Why do the turkeys belong to the women? Because it takes infinite pains and bother to raise them, no heavy work, no grand gestures with a team of mules or a double-bladed ax, just endless care and attention.

When, for example, the pullets get caught in a spring rain and their instincts do not advise them to go to shelter, it is the farm wife who builds a fire in the cookstove, dries each bird and warms it in the oven, who opens its tiny idiotic mouth and blows the breath of life into its lungs.

Besides, it is the wife who has protected those turkeys all summer not only from the foxes and skunks, but from the neighborhood agriculturists, including her husband, whose watermelon patches those turkeys had ogled all spring, until one day their chance came and they went into it and pecked holes in all the ripening melons.

She had chicken hens hatch out her turkey eggs, so that for a while at least the baby turkeys would follow the chickens instead of a mother of their own species who would literally have walked most of them to death. But while the baby turkeys did not have to keep up with the older turkeys, the farm wife did.

She has followed them hundreds of miles—ever on the alert for hawks, varmints, stray dogs that would kill fifty turkeys at a time for the fun of it. And she also watched for certain neighbors of easy morals and big appetites. For this herd of turkeys not only represents what warm clothes the family will be able to buy against the winter, it represents all of the farm woman's savings from last year. Every egg from which a turkey was or wasn't hatched cost her from twenty-five to fifty cents.

Ten years ago the post-oak lands would not have been so propitious a place for turkeys. It is true that the land was already sucked dry of whatever it had to give to cotton. The relevant thing is that the people were not yet convinced. Too many people still scratched at the sand and dropped cotton seed in it.

But ultimately poverty drove most of them away, and the use of the land fell to the quail and the foxes. The remaining farmers put out cattle to graze upon the unsucculent needle grass. The old houses on the abandoned land fell into a state of ruin greater than they'd ever known. And the time was ripe for the remaining farm women to raise turkeys.

There was room for them to range like sheep. In spring and summer the turkeys marched busily, tirelessly, over the abandoned fields in search of something that nothing else wanted: grasshoppers. They stalked these erstwhile pests, and greedily processed them into turkey meat. Then the first spring weeds began to go to seed, and here was grain no man had had either to plant or to cultivate, a present from God which the turkeys were glad to harvest.

On this diet, throughout the summer the turkeys grew tall and strong, wasting none of the yield of these broad free acres. For, while if used as range land for cattle, a fee would have had to be paid, a fence built, no owner of idle land would begrudge its yield of insects or weed seeds to a farm woman's turkeys.

But the greatest blessing of all was the falling of the rich manna of the post-oak trees themselves, the sea of acorns that covered the ground, acorns aplenty to fatten all the free-ranging hogs and turkeys that came forward to eat.

And then the Thanksgiving market opens and the question is whether to sell or hold till Christmas. The farm wife is almost too tired to decide. She has worried too much and walked too far. But when her husband suggests she hold for the Christmas market, she thinks of all the things that can happen to a turkey, all her fears of the summer, all the hard luck that has as yet been forestalled, and that the gods may not any longer be disposed to postpone.

"We're going to sell," she says, "and get the money in the bank. I'm tard o' traipsin' around and frettin' after those turkeys."

The turkeys will average ten pounds each. Suppose she has two hundred, and the price is twenty cents. That's four hundred dollars, say three-fifty net.

To gross that much her husband will have had to raise eight bales of ten-cent cotton. That will mean he's cultivated forty acres of sandy-land cotton, and had fair luck with the weather. His net profit will be half that of his wife's. Two hundred dollars. Whatever corn he's raised his own animals will eat. But it doesn't take any mules or equipment to raise turkeys. The wife, then, has that peculiar importance that comes to the greatest producer of wealth in the family.

But the family can earn still more money from their turkeys. They can pick at the packing plant when the kill begins. The family won't be too high-toned to do it either. Thirty cents an hour for each person picking runs into money when you've a family of five.

That's fifteen dollars for every ten hours' work, and that will buy a good second-hand cookstove, or three heavy wool mackinaws. So that's part of the deal with the turkey buyer. "We'll sell you our turkeys at the market price, if you'll save us five ropes at the kill."

That trade the buyer is delighted to make.

And on the night of the first kill—night because most of the pickers have other work to do in the day-time—the family gets into its spavined truck or its ten-year-old, sixth-hand car and comes to town.

The packing plant—at other seasons a warehouse for stock feed—is surrounded by wagons and trucks, women wearing sweaters and cook aprons, men in overalls, tattered leather jackets, old hunting caps with flaps over their cool ears. Those who could get them have on rubber boots. Trucks are continually arriving with coops of turkeys which are unloaded and weighed. And then the birds, according to their sex, are put into one of two large pens.

Negroes are going to pick too. They keep to themselves and out of the way as much as possible. The last thing on earth they want is trouble. They've got plenty as it is. But for some reason they are able to work at close quarters with white people at the turkey kills without any serious outbreaks. If any question comes up, the Negroes yield immediately, and if the white people are sober, that suffices.

The killer is a huge black man, the only skilled worker in the crowd. This afternoon he's made a trade with the boss. It was partly a boast, partly to receive certain cherished items.

"Boss man," he's said, "you know I kills fast and neat—faster than seventy ropes can pick. Ain't no use to have a man there with me to pull the tail and wing feathers. Just give me a half a pint o' Paul Jones whisky, a package of Camel cigarettes, an' my regular pay, and I'll kill and pull wing and tail feathers and not never get behind those pickers."

In most plants this is three men's work.

The boss has agreed.

When the kill begins, the man at the pen door takes a Tom turkey, hitches its feet to a short rope on an overhead conveyor, and gives it a push toward the killer. With a thin-bladed knife, razor sharp, the killer cuts the first throat on the inside, snatches out the wing and tail feathers, and sends the conveyor on with a push to the man who dunks the flopping turkey in hot water. He, in turn, scoots it on to a man beside a whirling, yard-in-diameter drum which is studded with soft rubber nibs. The turkey is held against these whirling nibs which clean off the bulk of the feathers. A waiting picker, actually finisher, then receives the more or less naked turkey, carries it to his rope suspended from the ceiling, and there completes the job, leaving a neat little ridge of pin feathers on the wing—for ornament and identification, since a man in California once sold dressed buzzards as turkeys.

The heads are wrapped neatly with paper. Then, without being drawn, the turkeys are put on racks and loaded into iced cars and started eastward.

They have now risen ten cents a pound in cost—the cost to the New York commission man. After he and the retailer have made a profit, the turkey, which brought twenty cents a pound alive, will retail, dressed, at thirty-eight.

But by the time the turkey is retailed, the Rockdale market will be closed. It will be Christmas, or past. The woman who raised your turkey will be sitting by the fire in a leaning house in the post-oak woods, perhaps listening to some orchestra playing at a New York hotel where an order of Texas Young Tom turkey brings two dollars and a half. She'll be enjoying herself hugely, snug by the fireplace, listening to a small radio set bought with her turkey money, while her husband, less attentive to the music, thinks of the cotton he will plant when the ground gets warm.

3

It's a good thing it don't rain as much in Milam County as it does in Houston. Did, bugs'd eat us up. We couldn't make any cotton at all. Then we *would* be in a fix.

It's cold in Central Texas after Christmas. Temperature drops sometimes to twenty. And there's never quite enough wood cut to carry you through these spells. What with cookin' and all. And so much raw north wind blowin' through the cracks in the walls, and up through the splintery floor. There may be one more hog to kill. And if there is, and your children are all too small to be much help, you invite a neighbor over to help hoist the singletree you've hooked into the hamstrings, to help scald and scrape and dress the carcass. Maybe he's got a good recipe for head cheese, or liver sausage. You might as well get some good out of him, because he's going to expect a thumping mess of spareribs and a bucket of lard for his trouble. Mind you, he's not charging you anything. But he'd think you were pretty cheap if you didn't give him anything, and you wouldn't blame him.

But if your hogs are all killed and you've got plenty of wood cut, which you won't have, you can hunt varmints at night if you've got a dog, or trap if you haven't, and make a little money out of the furs besides having a lot of sport. Of course you could hunt quail, but unless you can pot-shot the covey on the ground, it won't pay you in meat, and you'd better leave the quail shooting to the town fellows, who don't mind shooting up two bits' worth of cartridges to get one bird.

This is also good weather to sit around the domino parlor in town, and chew tobacco and watch the boys play who can afford to pay a nickel a game.

But mostly, it seems, you find yourself huddled around your own fireplace with the kids and dogs, trying to figure out what the signs, specially those in the almanac, predict for the coming crop year.

Because you're a cotton man, and so was your daddy and granddaddy, and everything hinges on that crop you're going to make soon as it's warm enough to plow and plant. You've got those old mortgages at the bank which have already been renewed three times, mortgages on your team and tools and next year's crop. This year you mean to whittle that mortgage down a little. Of course if cotton went sky high and the weather worked right, you might . . . well no telling what. But you'd settle for just a good average crop, by which you mean the kind you make one year out of four.

Anyway it won't be long now till corn planting time. Long about the end of February, when the land begins to warm, and the first little sprigs and bushes in the woods turn green.

But you got to plow that land first. Meant to get her busted last fall, but what with one thing and another it just slipped by. Specially since the cow got stopped up with that still-born calf.

But just let this weather fair off, and you'll hitch up those mules and bust that land. Too bad the mules are so poor right now, and getting so old. But they'll make it through if you don't carry 'em too fast and don't let the plow nose too deep in the ground.

Then almost before a cat can lick its behind, you'll have corn planted and up, and the weeds hoed out.

It's hard to keep from grinning right along here, when you realize how easy it is to sit by the fire in January and grow crops in your mind. But these things take a lot of figuring. And you might as well do some of it now.

What was that the landlord said about the government land, the part you get paid for not raising anything on? Oh, yes, said rent 'em that slough bottom again. Last year, just leaving it idle and drawing down the government money, the slough bottom brought in more money than any other part of the place.

But now that the corn's imagined planted, what about the real thing? The bolls full of long, spilling out white. What about the cotton?

You spit in the fire and it sizzles sharp and fine, and as that sound fades, it gives place to another in your mind: the click of the planter dropping seed in good soft earth that's been broken and harrowed. And then that little old cotton sticks its two green leaves out of the ground, all stiff and chipper and a bright blue-green.

If the March wind's been blowing peart, you may have to take time off to throw a little dirt against your corn stalks to keep 'em from getting blown loose in the ground. Then you grab up a hoe, and make the kids grab one too, and commence chopping that cotton, thinning stalks, killing weeds, making the rusty hoe-head bright. But it takes nearly as much time keeping those plague-taked kids on the job as it would to do all the chopping yourself. Your wife's about the only one you can chance turning your back on. Specially if one of the dogs has treed something down on the creek and the kids hear 'im barkin'.

Once choppin's done you plow that cotton out, and then kind of set back and get your breath. If the corn's not too tall, you can run a cultivator over it, and then you can really call yourself having laid by a crop. And if you feel like going to the creek for three or four days' catfishing, that's your business, because your conscience is clear and your crop's pretty clean.

Most likely by that time it's hot as hell, and the corn's suffering for want of rain. Maybe it's just plumb dried up and dead. Maybe not quite though, and you spend most of your time hoping at the sky, thinking what a difference a corn crop will make. Plenty of feed for the mules and hogs and chickens. Plenty of meal for cornbread. If it don't rain, you'll have to work your team and feed your hogs on bloodweeds, which is mighty poor, and get meal on credit at the store or from the Relief.

But it's only the corn you'll worry about, because the cotton will just wallow in the dry weather, and run long tap roots down to Jericho. It may turn dark green and sick-looking but it'll just be possuming, because all the cotton that couldn't stand dry weather died a long time ago and left no seed.

But if it's raining too much, that's another thing. Though the cotton may look happy and green, it doesn't really mean it. It's sick inside, and the boll weevils and the leaf worms are multiplying by the hurrying billions in the dark shade of its leaves.

At first, to fight 'em, you try plowing the dirt up into sharp hills under the plants so when the bugs fall off, they will roll down into the middles where the sun'll cook 'em and kill 'em.

If that doesn't work and it keeps on raining, you drive into town and buy poison. It costs like smoke but you've got it to do. There won't be much profit left in your crop. But it's you or the bugs now, and you didn't set out to grow a crop of bug feed.

But after all you're just sitting by the fireplace imagining, maybe pulling a thick splinter off the floor and whittling it slowly, savingly, and dreaming. It doesn't matter about the floor because the old house is about to fall down anyway. The landlord doesn't fix it because he says the next feller—and there'll most likely be another one all right next year—will want something different, and the place probably not show a profit anyway, so why fool with it? And you guess that makes sense from his end of the line.

But since you're just sittin' here figgering, you aren't really going to believe in boll weevils and floods and drouths. You got troubles enough without hunting 'em up. You figger never trouble trouble, till trouble troubles you. If you didn't kind of count on things getting a little better, you'd have give up the ghost long ago. What with all the hard luck you've had with crops, and the trouble the kids got into, and so much sickness. So to hell with hard luck, you figure.

What about the fun you're going to have? Never a year but you had some. What about all the house dances, and baptizin's and funerals? What about the cemetery workings after the crop's laid by, when you pack a lunch, and meet the other neighborhood folks at the cemetery, and hoe out the weeds, and each tombstone or wooden marker brings up old stories of fighting and drinking and making love, of big crops, and better days? See folks there you'd never see anywhere else. Unless it's maybe at the poultry show.

But the laid-by lull doesn't last forever. There's corn to be topped and gathered. And then comes cotton picking time.

Maybe your land's not bottom land this year, so there's no danger from floods, and your crop's small enough for your family to pick by Christmas. In that case you don't need to hire your picking done.

But the big fellows will, and a happy, loud-talkin' excitement will be felt in all the Negro sections of the towns.

Now they'll get their chance to earn some money, to clean up a few back debts, to buy a few clothes.

Maybe you don't like Negroes much. Lots of times, in winter, when you try to get day-labor jobs they beat you to them, and that leads to bad feeling. But now, the thought of fields full of Negroes picking cotton warms you a little. Even if you have never given them anything, they give you a little something now, a little pleasure. Because that field full of working Negroes is one of the livingest sights you ever saw. It's like a hungry man eatin' hearty. It's like an animal, long in heat, being bred. It's full of a people with a feeling for the earth's bigness and richness and wonderment, coming back to it after a year of the emptiness of town. It is a sad sight, and a happy sight. In a way it's kind of a holy one.

But those Negroes to you are just part of the furniture of harvest time. What you are interested in is getting the cotton picked and in the wagon, and if you're hiring it picked, seeing that none of the pickers put any rocks in the sacks since you're paying fifty cents per hundred pounds.

And now that cotton must be ginned, and all roads lead to town.

Something that started with a lot of careful figuring beside a January fire, and that went on through the breaking of land (maybe poor land, but land), and the planting of seed, has finished up, one way or another.

And something that can be seen and used—something folks need to keep from going naked and cold—has been made.

Maybe you're broke, and disappointed because you are so broke, but it still feels pretty good.

You've made a crop er cotton, and by God, that's something!

5. Ranch Country

ONE of our most threadbare stories tells of a Texas miner in the Klondike gold rush arising one morning and going outside to look at his thermometer. Back inside, he shivered, then turning to his partner said, "Fifteen below this morning, Bill. An' if it's that cold here, there just ain't no tellin *how* cold it is in Amarillo."

There are other stories to the effect that the rest of us in Texas look upon the Panhandle people as Yankees. As a matter of fact, some of us do, which is not unreasonable when you recall that Amarillo is some seven hundred and seventy miles north of Brownsville.

The Panhandle is that northern outcropping of Texas which juts into, and might just as well have been,

Oklahoma. In a way we're sort of apologetic about its size, since it has an area of only some fifteen thousand square miles. Originally there was lots more room up there. But the state government, being hard up in 1850, peddled close to a hundred thousand square miles of this territory to the United States for ten million dollars. As a matter of fact, that seems to have represented the general policy of the Texas government in those days: Take the cash, the railroads, the public buildings, and let the land go. Nevertheless, a noticeable amount of the state was left, and that northern extension called the Panhandle is ramrodded by the city of Amarillo.

Amarillo is populated by some forty-eight thousand wind-blown, sand-stung souls who, with the myopia of love, look upon this land as God-chosen. To them their city, and the advancement thereof, is a sacred cause, and their high priest is Gene Howe, editor of the Amarillo *Globe* and *Daily News*. This contingent, though perhaps at the moment covered up in flying dust, officially regards the Dust Bowl as the devilish invention of Eastern journalists. Yet it is difficult even for such zealots as these to shout into oblivion the memorable lines of a German farmer who'd got enough of the Panhandle and was checking out. "De vedder out here," he laconically remarked, "I do not like. De rain vas all vind, and de vind vas all sand."

Nevertheless, in good years, the Panhandle makes some thirty of Texas' thirty-five million bushels of wheat. It makes five per cent of Texas' cotton. And like so many other parts of Texas it is not without subterranean riches. Here are some four thousand plus oil wells; also, the biggest natural gas field in the world, with the tidy estimated reserve of twenty-four trillion cubic feet.

But something had to give way, had to make room for the wheat and cotton and oil fields of the Panhandle, and that something was cattle. Consequently, the cattlemen have been the chief "I-told-you-so-ers" in the matter of the Dust Bowl. "God," they point out, "never meant the land to be plowed." Yet ranching has by no means vanished. The second biggest ranch in Texas still operates here: The Matador Land and Cattle Company, Ltd., a Scottish syndicate, controlling 860,000 acres on which it runs 52,000 head of cattle.

There are many other big cow ranches in this section, but the goat and sheep country lies to the southeastward on the Edwards Plateau, a vast limestone mesa the size of Tennessee. Its capital, 315 miles from Amarillo, is the town of San Angelo.

The Edwards fills forty Texas counties and is the best sheep and goat country in the nation. Not all land will raise goats. If it is damp or flat, their hoofs quickly begin to be seriously affected. The Edwards, of course, is by no means damp. It is rocky, broken country, but its shallow top soil, rich in the proper minerals, is covered with buffalo grass, with oak, mesquite, and juniper—and this shrubbery is much to the point, because goats, it frequently appears, would rather dine reared up on their hind legs, tearing leaves and twigs out of a tree, than on all four feet cropping grass. A steer can utilize only forty-five per cent of the range grasses; a sheep uses sixty-five. An old goat, however, dispatches with relish eighty-five per cent of whatever grows out of the ground—just about everything, that is, except tree trunks. That, in fact, is one of the principal reasons for the existence of Texas' goat- and sheep-raising industry, when, no matter how you look at it, cattle ranching has so much more *éclat*.

Sheep and goats are not, generally speaking, as durable as cattle. An early freezing norther soon after the fall clip may kill an entire herd. But woe betide the rattlesnake that so much as cocks a snoot at a goat. Into the air goes William, traveling on hind feet, using the sharp front feet as lances. He will chop that snake to pieces in a jiffy. Incidentally, a deer will do the same, while a range hog, his shield of fat keeping the venom out of his bloodstream, will often devour his presumptuous attacker tail first.

The chief function of the sheep and goat men's association is to keep foreign produce similar to theirs off of the American market, but it also carries on a running-fire engagement with the Texas fox and wolf hunters over what view a rancher is entitled to take toward a sheep-killing dog.

Most cowmen, unless they happen to be raising a few sheep themselves, look upon a sheep rancher not only as a person of little pride, but as an agent of the devil, and back in the free-range days blows and bullets were frequently exchanged between them. For while a herd of cattle will graze at random, a herd of sheep will denude the earth of grass as it grazes, preferring to crop closer and walk less. And since any real cattleman looks upon the range as the source of all blessings present and future, he could hardly be expected to lie down with the sheep man in anything less than a double grave.

West of the sheep country there yet remains another vast realm combining the Big Bend (contained inside the huge swinging turn of the Rio Grande) and the Trans-Pecos country. Here are the Bad Lands, mountains (the Davis range, which is a spur of the Rockies), canyons, desert, cactus, greasewood, Spanish dagger, sagebrush. Here is where Texas travels farthest west and then dies of thirst. A citizen of this section, when asked how much it rained here, replied simply, "Mister, hit don't." It is said of this country that everything either "stings, sticks, or stinks."

Yet here again is oil. Nineteen years ago, "hamboning" along on almost no money at all, a candy salesman sank a well that brought in the West Texas fields. One lease hound for a major company, having at hand very little time and a two-million-dollar drawing account, leased four counties almost solidly more or less overnight.

Built around the edge of a mountain, El Paso, with 108,000 people, is the metropolis of this section. And El Paso is no sissy. It is a town of miners, ranchers, cavalrymen, and straight tequila. This is the locality of Owen P. White's *Lead and Likker*, etc. It's also the home of Tom Lea, the artist and illustrator.

Here the Elephant Butte irrigation project has opened

up 180,000 acres of desert land to fruit and vegetable culture. And it has an advantage over the lower Rio Grande areas in that it gets first whack at the precious water, and because, properly watered, its bottom lands will raise such appalling yields as two or three bales of cotton to the acre.

These are the lonesome lands: the Big Bend, the Trans-Pecos, the Edwards Plateau, and the Panhandle, where a few men move over great distances. These millions of sparsely settled acres are the Texas frontiers. And there is still another: what the Mexicans call the Monte, or the Brasada, what we Texans know as the Brush Country.

Draw a line from Del Rio on the Mexican border up to San Antonio and thence southeastward to the Gulf of Mexico, and there you will have the Monte—home of the greatest cattle herds on earth, of the biggest rattlers, tarantulas, scorpions, and horned toads. Yet were you to drive through it tomorrow on a trip from San Antonio to Laredo, you'd probably see not a fourth as many cows as you would on a long summer drive in Wisconsin. That is because rain and grass are scarce in the Monte. The usual concentration of cattle per hundred acres runs from as many as ten head, to as few as two, so that unless you see a few head of cattle gathered around a water hole, you may very easily get the idea that the great herds are a myth. The trouble is there is so much room. A ranch of 100,000 acres is by no means, from a quantitative standpoint, "a braggin' ranch." A 300,000-acre ranch is a little more respectable. Tops for size, is, of course, the King Ranch in deep South-west Texas. The best gauge to how much land it really contains is the fact that there is a month's difference in the seasons between the southern and northern portions of the ranch. But of this empire, more anon.

SOME POINTERS ON HOW TO, AND NOT TO, RUN A RANCH

Lil Dimmitt was the youngest mayor Georgetown, Texas, ever had, and the hardest luck cow rancher in the history of Texas. Lil is now one of the football coaches, and chief proselytizer of athletic talent, for Texas A. and M. College, but as a young man Lil had a patrimony and a yen to become a rancher.

He decided to go at the matter "right." On a peak market he bought the best (not the largest) ranch to be found and the finest stock money could buy—registered sows costing two hundred dollars a head, registered cattle and sheep and goats.

Well, in the quickest possible time, everything that could go wrong did, and in the ranching business everything can. First there was a drouth that killed his feed crop, withered his range, and exhausted his watering places. Next, livestock prices dropped to subterranean levels. Finally, because the ticks were bad, he bathed each of his fine cattle with creosote dip by hand. But since he'd neglected to dilute the creosote properly with water, each of the cattle promptly died. Now he was forced to sell his remaining property. His hogs, which had greedily devoured a crop of corn and were "rolling" fat, brought him one-third of what he'd paid for them originally. And all that a ranch itself will bring from a prospective buyer at these periods is a look of scorn. In no time at all then, Lil was flat broke.

I've seen other people go broke in the cow business in three months, but usually it takes a little longer, especially for the people who were brought up in the ranching business. They've got the feel, the know-how, and most of the new money in the business finally accrues to these old hands.

Two of the oldest ranching families in Texas are the Kings and the Kenedys. Much of South Texas that the King Ranch doesn't occupy, the Kenedy Ranch does.

The King Ranch came into existence in 1851 when old Richard King, traveling with Robert E. Lee, selected the Santa Gertrudis site (one ranch in the contemporary King system) and went into the cow business. Mifflin Kenedy, a pal of King's and erstwhile partner (they had run a supply boat to Mexico), went into the same business on a near-by ranch, which was to become the second biggest ranch in South Texas.

At present the King Ranch comprises a million and a quarter acres of land and the appurtenances necessary to a domain of that size. It is managed by the Klebergs (a Kleberg married Captain King's daughter), and it is not an overstatement to say they are literally ranching hell out of it.

> The sun's done riz and the sun's done set
> An' I ain't offen the King Ranch yet.

In many ways the King Ranch is unique, yet it is probably Texas' most representative institution. Like

Texas, it is the biggest of its kind, almost violently progressive, marked by some dissension, full of vinegar, and making money.

The "little pasture" of the King Ranch is 6,000 acres. Three others are 65,000 acres each. The family has its own representative in the United States Congress, but the government of the ranch itself, despite a board of directors, is seated between Bob Kleberg, Jr.'s, ears. Bob Kleberg is a super-charged individual, and it follows that the King Ranch is a super-charged business.

Though the Klebergs are horse-riding, gun-toting, genuine ranch folk, the ranch has been mechanized and organized to the hilt. Lesser methods could hardly keep its gigantic processes in flux. For example, a spring shipment of 17,000 head (shipping charges: $100,000) could not be profitably shipped to market without the most careful timing and efficiency, since every delay means a loss in weight of valuable beef. For one thing, the King loaders use electric prods for quickening the pace of sluggard animals in the loading pens and chutes.

Among other latter-day ranching gadgets now in use on the King Ranch is an imported Argentine corral. Into this maze-like device a young bull may enter with a singing heart and no suspicions. When he leaves it a few minutes later, he has been pumped full of vaccine, his burning rump is fresh-branded, his noble horns sawed off, and worst of all, he isn't a bull any more. It's happened so fast that he doesn't know what hit him, even though there is no question in his mind as to whether he *was* hit.

There are portable mechanisms that go down a fence line drilling every post so that the barbed wire may be tied rather than stapled to the post.

There are "bump" gates, which swing open on being lightly struck with a car bumper, pause a moment for a car to pass through, then close.

A great, drag-line-looking gadget with a gargantuan hammer claw on its end rips mesquite trees out of the earth on pasture-clearing projects.

Too, the ranch has its own pasture-crossing motor vehicles: light cars with most of the body cut away and with elevated rear seats so that persons sitting on them may shoot over the head of the driver. In these cars, a half dozen rifles and assorted pistols are standard equipment. The car itself is not entirely without kinship to the American Army's jeeps. Filling stations are scattered at reasonable distances over the vast pastures.

And this is the direction in which ranching, like so many other businesses which have thus far resisted it, must inevitably move—toward mechanization, particularly in the machining of great distances into little ones.

The King Ranch incorporates most of the kinds of land to be found in the state, from coastal marsh to desert, which gives it a good jockeying position in its conflict with the elements. When drouth strikes its inland domains, there will be grass of a kind on its coastal ranges. Surrounding its various pastures there are 1,500 miles of fence.

Its cow hands, unlike those in the Panhandle who are Anglo-Saxon and those around Beaumont who are chiefly French boys and Negroes, are Mexican *vaqueros*.

These King *vaqueros* are in a sense a *corps d'élite* among ranch hands, unquestionably the proudest men I ever saw. You feel at once that they would not trade places with anyone else on earth and that they look upon ordinary mortals, those, that is, who do not ride for the Kings, as clearly inferior to themselves.

Were this fealty of the "boughten" variety, it would be less remarkable. The astounding fact is that all this enthusiasm concerns a dollar-a-day job plus mounts and found.

Not only are these Mexicans handy with a lariat; the carbine and the six-shooter are no strangers to them. Cattle rustlers (the present-day version is a man and his partner in a fast truck, loading at night, butchering en route, and selling the meat to distant retailers at daylight) are likely to find that nocturnal egress from the King domain is less a probability than is sudden death from the skillfully fired six-shooter of a King *vaquero*.

The abundant game inside the ranch is apt to lure zealous nimrods over the fence, wherein some have vanished. And if no absolute cause can be established, the ranch neighbors may unofficially give credit to the King game wardens. Too, since the non-ranch and ranch people have antipathetic political interests, particularly where land taxes—the great bugaboo of ranching—are concerned, an occasional misunderstanding is, perhaps, to be expected.

As yet, however, open warfare has not been declared between the ranch and Texas, even though in the past the ranch did exist in a state of undeclared war with a good many Mexican bandits for a good many years.

As this is written, all ranchers in Texas are coining money. First threats of war, then war itself, drove cattle prices to thumping highs. Though 1941 was a drouth year for most of the nation, Texas was inundated And there is an old saying that if it rains in July and August, it doesn't matter in Texas who's president of the United States. Tall grass and high prices make the rancher's position perfect. Without the rain and grass, he might have to flood the market with untenable herds. With plenty of grass he finds himself in a position to hoard his wares and protect the price.

It is also said that every cowman goes broke three times in a life span. For many that is true—lack of rain, a disastrous price, or inadequate financial reserves, any one of them can bust a rancher. Usually it's all three at once.

But the King Ranch has taken these dangers into account. It has assured supplies of water (two hundred and sixty-five windmills with five windmill maintenance crews). It has proved that it can make profits on a low beef price (in 1932, at depression prices, the ranch made an operating profit of $400,000) and as beef prices rise, ranch profits increase geometrically rather than mathematically, since most ranching costs are fixed costs, such as taxes and labor. One cow hand can manage as many hundred-dollar cows as ten-dollar ones, and the expensive ones won't eat any more grass than the cheap ones.

Finally, the King Ranch, for all its experiments, modernization, and mechanized equipment purchases, is probably threatened by no debt burden at all. At one time King Ranch paper (open notes) was regarded almost as legal tender in Texas. But it is rumored that the last three million dollars the ranch owed has been placed with the Humble Oil Company on a twenty-year basis, as one consideration in a lease deal wherein the ranch land en masse was leased to the Humble (owned by Standard) for thirteen cents per acre per year.

And while most of our smaller ranchers may lack the organizing ability of the King management and have less fortuitous credit arrangements, all Texas ranchers, however unscientific their approach, know cows—the temperaments of the different breeds, what, in a sudden crisis, say a stampede, is going to develop even before it happens—and some of them are the most creative breeders to be found. Their hunches grow out of so much experience and understanding that "hunches" is the wrong word altogether.

The ranch people in Texas, for some reason, actually tend toward an especial tallness and leanness. The cattlemen's personalities and mental processes are generally straightforward and forceful.

The legend that cow hands are silent men is, I think, only partially true. Many of them, when sober, are embarrassed by the presence of strangers. But armed with a jolt or two of Bourbon whisky, most of them will talk your ears off. After downing two or three more, they are apt to want to go bust a bronc.

A rancher's hat is usually about three-quarters of the size of that of a movie cowboy. His high-heeled boots are ordinarily plain black leather with fancy stitching in colored thread, and the tops a couple of inches taller than those affected by rodeo hands and actors. It is perhaps one of the vagaries of the Texas mind that I like Coke Stevenson better because his boots are of this old West variety, instead of the more rakish, low-cut type, which, now that I think of it, my own are.

If the ranching Texan has on his everyday work clothes, which he greatly prefers to all others, he will be wearing brown canvas pants with brass rivets at every seam-turn or corner. To button a pair of those pants when they are brand new is the finger-bustingest job I know of, because the reinforced buttonholes are stiff as iron. Our Texan's brown shirt will be open at the throat, his skin a deep-tanned russet, his hands tough as rawhide, his legs not bowed but straight. Over his shirt he will wear a brush jacket of the same cast-iron canvas of which his trousers are made, and he wouldn't be caught dead in a pair of overalls.

Of all this gear, his pride is involved only in his boots and hat. The handmade boots he wears cost a minimum of twenty dollars (he'd rather wear work shoes than ready-made boots) and his hat cost fifteen. The remainder of his clothes probably cost five dollars in all.

His leather chaps and spurs are up behind the seat of his pick-up truck. In the trailer he has a saddled horse to be unloaded and ridden when the truck has gone as far as it can. Why the cowman has quit wearing his spurs in town, I don't know, unless it is that they would interfere with the foot acceleration of an automobile. When I was a boy, I could always tell by the merry jingle of spurs when an unseen cow hand was approaching. Another thing that is no longer seen is the plaited rawhide quirt. They aren't even advertised any more in the mail order catalogues.

But to us Texans there is a quality of go and glamor about cowmen that farmers never attain. I don't know what makes it. Is it the fact that they ride horses? That probably has something to do with it. But I am led for some reason to believe that it is the cowman's mixture of pride and arrogance—plus his knowledge that he has casually put something over on the rest of us. For while the rancher goes through the violent motions of labor, he is actually having a wonderful time earning a living; doing something he would of spiritual necessity have had to do anyway for the good of his own soul, in order to live up to his own concepts of freedom and dignity. Perhaps that's it, that the ranchers are the last free men in a swiftly industrializing America, and that they become thereby a noble and enviable symbol of what so many of the rest of us have eternally lost.

6. City Slickers

OF TEXAS' six and a half million scattered inhabitants, about a million live in four Texas cities: Dallas, Fort Worth, Houston and San Antonio, Dallas and San Antonio each having a quarter of a million, Houston a third, Fort Worth a sixth.

Little Austin, on the Colorado River, named after Stephen Austin and containing the great university of which he dreamed, is Texas' capital city. It's an extremely pretty town of 90,000 people. Its streets are wide, its terrain sharply rolling.

Its leading store is Scarbrough's, which was built up by those Rockdale Scarbroughs. As you walk up

Congress Avenue, the next noteworthy object is the Stephen F. Austin Hotel, which is rather a nice little hotel except for the perennial and somehow demoralizing collection of flea-bitten legislators who loaf in its lobby. A few blocks on up the street is the capitol, which is elsewhere described. And a half mile or so farther on is big and rich Texas University, which has latterly begun to build itself skyscrapers, since living space is so restricted in Texas.

The bastion of North Central Texas, its queen city and brightest jewel, is Dallas-on-the-Trinity, the effulgent and lovely Athens of the alfalfa fields, where what is commonly regarded as civilization has made its greatest strides in Texas.

When the Metropolitan Opera Company goes on tour, it makes one stop in Texas. That is at Dallas. And opening night is a spectacle, the glories of which tax the pen. Out of the moth balls come Texas tail coats. Our oil aristocracy snaps to attention. Photographers go out from the Dallas *News* with firm instructions that the sky's the limit. Its entertainment critic, John Rosenfeld, drops his workaday monicker of dictator of "the lively arts" and straightens up his face. Limousines streak into town from the Houston and San Antonio highways—the big pot is in the little one. *Ars gratia artis* and a new dress from Neiman-Marcus that will lend itself well to society column description become the order of the day.

Which, in a sense, is sort of nice. What's the use in

having big shots if they won't shell out for such genuinely worth-while though expensive baubles as the
opera? We plainer citizens grow atingle reading the
breathless news stories. For we are surfeited with local
larceny and quotations from the green hide market.
(Life without culture is hard, brother.)

But hardly has Dallas's pulse begun to return to
normal after the departure of the opera company, until
the advance man for the *corps de ballet* lands in town,
and up again goes the old fever chart. The Dallas *News*
is smeared with double-page spreads of bounding
danseurs and *-euses*—and when the performances start,
there'll be packed houses and responsive audiences.

Once in New York I was in a roomful of leaping,
samovar-rushing, name-calling ballet people, and when
the word got out that I was a Texan, I became a kind of
hero.

"Ah, Dallas!" they sighed. "It's the best tour stop
that we make. Such wonderful audiences! Such wonderful publicity!"

But chiefly they thought of Texas as a man named
Rosenfeld, surrounded by a large body of land and
eager ticket purchasers.

With books it is the same. Dallas buys more books
than the rest of the state combined, and the welcome
mat is always out to visiting practitioners of the
literary arts and rackets. In this friendly town when the
chicken is passed, it is not the preacher but the visiting
littérateur who gets the white meat.

As a matter of fact, Dallas is not without capable

writers of its own. The heavyweight champ in the Dallas literary scene is John McGinnis, of the English department at Southern Methodist University, editor of the *Southwest Review*. In the same department is Dr. Beatty, critic, author, and technician of the drama. Too, there are Wayne Gard, biographer, and Sam Acheson, political historian and Boswell to the Dallas *News*. Also resident in Dallas are two of the nation's crack magazine writers, Norma Patterson and Helen Topping Miller.

Sometime ago a great schism arose among the Dallas literati when Henry Smith, a brilliant young English professor of S. M. U. and a critic of parts, wrote an introduction to a special subscription edition of a Faulkner book which one faction considered naughty.

Still another art flourishes in this many-times-blessed community, and that is the art of dressing milady fit to kill. The materials, elegant as any obtainable in America, lie readily at hand at Neiman-Marcus's, a store which is without peer along the reaches of Fifth Avenue or Fifty-seventh Street.

Before the war this superlative establishment maintained its own corps of buyers abroad and bought copiously and well of Paris originals, which its statewide clientele snapped up like hot cakes. And the difference between its salespeople and those of an ordinary high-quality department store is the difference between a politician and a statesman. A casual visitor who doesn't want to buy anything, but just to look at the store, gives the salespeople great pleasure—

through the agency of their humble offices they have the privilege, they feel, of offering the visitor a distinguished and memorable experience.

Dallas makes its money through finance and wholesaling consumer goods. It also contains a bumper crop of state supervisors and branch executives for Eastern companies. But the thing that makes it Dallas, that makes it a dignified go-getter, a patron of the arts, a nerve center in the battle against cotton and associated reactionary influences in Texas, is its definitely patrician and intelligent quotidian, the Dallas *News*.

I feel that the *News* is a great paper because it has immense institutional pride and *esprit de corps*, an outstandingly capable staff, and a kind of Olympian arrogance of viewpoint. If the *News* thinks it's right on an issue, it feels, at least privately, that for the people of Texas to disagree is simply evidence of their appalling cheek and bad taste.

Some Texas journalists think the *News* ("the oldest business institution in Texas") is more discreet than courageous. But in the old days, it was not afraid to pour fire on the sensitive tail of Sam Houston. Nor later was it afraid to endorse Jim Ferguson when the disheartening choice was between Ferguson and the Ku Klux Klan. It also went down with all guns blazing at the Prohibition bogey.

The *News* considers itself the spokesman not only for Dallas, but for Texas, and where the interests of Texas are concerned, the *News* won't hold its fire. You can look at the president, G. B. Dealey, a distinguished gentleman of eighty-four, who in his time has been something of a second Stephen Austin, and know at once that he wouldn't play that way.

Suppose you were sitting in a Texas draw poker game, had bet your shirt on three eights, and it was time to show the cards. If your opponent, when asked what he held, used the common expression "From Dallas to Fort Worth," you would be out of luck. He'd have three tens. The distance between those cities is thirty miles.

Fort Worth, in its relations with Dallas, has much the psychology of a poor but belligerent relative. Its first citizen, by decibel rating in particular, is the energetic ten-gallon-hat-giving publisher, Amon Carter. Its slogan is "Where the West Begins," and its business is butchery—for here are located the great, stinking packing plants that process Texas cattle into food.

It is a big-hearted, loud-mouthed city which won't take the supremacy of Dallas lying down. When Texas held its centennial celebration in 1936 and spent many million dollars on its exposition in Dallas, that was too much for Fort Worth. At once Fort Worth sent for Billy Rose, told him to shoot the works on his "Casa Mañana," and plastered the state with posters which said: "Go to Dallas for education. Come to Fort Worth for entertainment."

In many ways Fort Worth comes nearer expressing the spirit of the state than any other Texas city.

Until old W. T. Waggoner died, he was the local nabob both in matters fiscal and bovine. But in his heart he was a rancher, and that was all he wanted to be. He was running 60,000 head of cattle on a half million acres of North Texas land, when a driller outraged him by bringing in an oil well on this land. "Damn it," "Pappy" Waggoner said, "cattle can't drink that stuff." Incidentally, this was the discovery well of the great Electra field.

When Mr. Waggoner died in 1934, he was allegedly worth around a hundred million dollars. Yet when the Waggoner Building was constructed, he refused to set his hand to a million-dollar check to pay for it. "You sign it," he said to his banker. "It don't seem right for a man to sign a check for that much money."

Fort Worth's slogan might be more accurately worded if it said, "Where the West is fixin' to get ready to begin." For the farmers have moved onto the "Grand Pray-ree" and crowded most of the ranchers farther west.

Fort Worth is akin to Houston only in the fact that jug-jowled Jesse Jones owns sizable chunks of both— though the Jones interests in Houston are many times more extensive, so far as anybody knows. For Jesse's managers talk only to Jesse, and Jesse talks only to God. It is known that Jesse owns a few million dollars' worth of Houston hotels and also that he owns the Houston *Chronicle*. But there are other juicy items in the town that Jesse might have a use for, whose ownership and control are matters of conjecture. I mean they get in tight places and borrow a few millions, but nobody knows who holds the mortgages, though it's anybody's guess. A Jonesian preference seems to be for controlling five hundred inter-related, profit-bearing ventures rather than owning fifty outright.

In any case the town is divided on the Jones issue. His innumerable competitors say they haven't got a chance. But most of the town is probably pro-Jones for the tangible reason that whatever his motives might have been, he has done a great deal for the municipal welfare.

And Houston has grown and prospered in magical degree since the time old Sam named it after himself and declared it capital of the state—a declaration that didn't stick because the Austinites refused to relinquish the state records. (When certain of Houston's early civic zealots tried to steal those records in the dark of night, the Austinites opened fire and drove off the invaders.)

If someone had told Sam that eventually his inland city would harbor great ocean-going vessels, he'd probably have snorted and said what he did at the party when he spat out a mouthful of burning-hot rice pudding on the table: "Many a fool would have swallowed that."

But that miracle was wrought. Buffalo Bayou was dredged across fifty miles of prairie to Galveston Bay. And the ships that had always stopped at Galveston Island passed it by and discharged their cargoes at Houston. In two decades, starting absolutely from scratch, Houston surpassed all other Texas ports and became the third seacoast port in tonnage in the United

States. That is somewhat understandable if you consider the statement of the doubtless modest Chamber of Commerce that Houston's trade territory equals the combined areas of Massachusetts, New Jersey, New Hampshire, Vermont, Maryland, Connecticut, Rhode Island, and the District of Columbia. Meanwhile the island city of Galveston began, for all its bravely blossoming oleanders, to show signs of age and fatigue.

But not only did Houston receive a transfusion of sea water. Oil began to be discovered everywhere about her. Oil capital flooded her banks, refinery payrolls her department stores. Her outskirts were covered with hundreds of acres of oil field equipment companies.

Houston people like to say that Dallasites invest in cars and clothes, Houstonians in homes. Maybe there's something in it, though Dallasites no more live in tents than Houstonians go naked. But it is true that Houston's bigwig reservation, River Oaks, is a real estate development of much beauty and swank.

Houston, however, like the man it was named for and the man who owns it, is not so much Texan as American. It has lost its Texas character by outgrowing Texas. It has taken on a great deal of the non-regional aspect of an adding machine, of big, but colonial finance. The place is full of foreigners from the United States, who are perfectly all right but just aren't Texans. Rice Institute might be Yale except for differences in architecture and in the potency of their football teams. The standards of scholarship are equally high and uncompromising.

Houston's waterfront is any waterfront, while Galveston's, for example, is Galveston's, as Marseille's is Marseille's.

Houston's stores are any city's stores. So, more or less, are her other properties, with one exception: the Rice Hotel, which is something about which Texans feel something.

But a delinquency in individuality is a charge that can never be laid upon the stone and adobe ramparts of San Antonio. First, it is an impostor. It is an ancient Spanish city pretending to be American. But it really isn't pretending very hard. The Army's Eighth Corps Area headquarters quadrangle at Fort Sam Houston might just as well have been built by a Spanish colonial army. The Mexican quarter, which isn't very definite, is genuinely and unmistakably Mexican beyond anything anybody can do about it. The railroad stations resemble eggs laid by a Mexican eagle. The streets, happy-go-lucky Mexican style, make no sense whatever. At night a great spread of red-cloth-covered tables fans out from the market place, and here Mexican women sell tamales. Guitar-strumming minstrels serenade the customers. And it's all on the level. With only minor interruptions, this institution has been in operation for a couple of hundred years.

It is to this market that the year-round stream of trucks from the Lower Rio Grande Valley brings that portion of the Valley produce that Texas can absorb. Here the peak activity is at two o'clock in the morning, as the truckloads of lettuce, of tomatoes, of every kind of vegetable and fruit, pass from the Valley truckers to the hundreds of drivers who will move out over Texas, leaving a crate or two in front of each as-yet-unopened grocery store on his route.

But the market place is not the only lively spot at two o'clock in the morning. Many San Antonians who have no connection at all with the market will still be aprowl, whooping it up and enjoying themselves, for San Antonio is traditionally a glad-time town. When the soldiers come in on payday, when the rancher comes in from his ranch, frolic is not only in order but does ensue.

Some years ago uplift invaded this hitherto easy-going city. The Rangers came to town and literally busted up the bars and gambling houses. They even went so far as to attack the restricted area. Appalled by this state of affairs, one San Antonian, whose grandfather had been prominent in high Confederate councils of war, remarked with grief, "It will take the most circumspect preparations to repair the damage."

In a lesser sense San Antonio is a genuinely glamorous and romantic city. You really feel those things, even in the daytime. But that's not what you feel most. The main thing is serious and lies deep in the earth, and that is brutality.

This is the town of the Spanish soldier—of the siesta and the bayonet. The stamp of the butcher, of His Excellency, General Santa Anna, is still there. The feeling of "orders," of military regulations, of glazed-eyed top sergeants—all these things, inflexible and brutal, as opposed to intelligence, one feels there. This is the town of the hard-drinking regular. This heart-chilling sensation comes to you with great eloquence out of the cannon-battered ramparts of the old forts and missions, out of the shabby, steamy whore cribs along Matamoros Street.

Yet it is only the feeling, and not the fact, for now the heart of this old city sings a prancing, high-keyed tune. It has been re-invaded by the spiritual descendants of that magnificent gang of clerks, college boys, and generally unmilitary souls who went down fighting and yelling and tearing Mexicans' ears off at the somewhat unprepossessing little piece of Spanish architecture across the plaza from the present-day post office: the Alamo. The new invaders are the definitely non-siesta-taking lads in the Air Corps.

If ever the good Lord collected a handsomer, more intelligent and determined group of fighters, their whereabouts are not known to me. They are, whether drilling, drinking, flying or courting, the most stirring sight I have ever seen.

But in addition to the Air Corps, San Antonio has another distinction that should not go unsung to a transient world, and that is the beautiful, and in every way sumptuous, St. Anthony Hotel. The cadets hive at the Gunter, but of all the hotels in Texas, in fact all in the world where I have stayed, none is more comfortable and few more beautiful than the St. Anthony, where in the late afternoon a Mexican string trio soothes the nerves of tight-corseted, Guernsey-busted dowagers in its great and pleasantly ornate lobby. And its Anacacho Room, named, I believe, after the owner's ranch (the room where dining and dancing and a certain sedate tippling is done), is filled not only with Army officers and wrought-iron grille work, but seems to be blessed with a singularly comely female clientele. What particularly intrigues me is that the lights in the rooms don't snap off or on. You push a wall switch with your finger, but it just glides without passing over the customary little bump. And, oddly enough, the St. Anthony is not especially expensive.

Finally, if you're in the shoe business, you might like to know that San Antonio is the greatest dumping ground for women's out-size shoes in the nation. Mexican women, you see, have small narrow feet, and many of them haven't much money. Almost no shoe is too small or narrow for them and, owing to financial necessity, no extremely cheap shoe can be too large.

So, if you have a little foot, or want to eat tamales in the open air to a guitar serenade, or sleep in a wonderful hotel, the place to go is San Antonio.

7. Things Peculiarly Our Own

$\mathcal{M}$OST ANYTHING that is indigenous to the Southwest we feel belongs exclusively to Texas. The fact, of course, is that it doesn't. But that's the way our minds work.

Take the jack rabbit for instance. Though he is common to the entire Southwest, we look upon him as a Texas invention, are proud of how fast he can run and how long his ears are. We are thrilled by the sight of an old jack waltzing across a needlegrass field at twenty or thirty miles an hour, ears straight up and taking it easy. At this gait, he can outrun most dogs. But when the greyhounds jump him, he hauls in those wind-resisting ears, straightens out, and, as a colored friend of mine says, "raley zizzes."

So, too, is the blue quail peculiarly our own. The northern and central parts of the state have a fine and thriving population of bob-white quail, but so do

many other states. The Mexican blue is another matter—
half bird, half jack rabbit. A bird dog may strike their
trail, come very near to them and point, but when the
hunter arrives, the dog will be pointing where the quail
were, instead of where they are. For blue quail are
like time and tide. The best way to hunt them is in a
track suit and on an empty stomach. It's the footwork
that counts.

In the blue quail country the rattlesnakes abound and
prosper in a degree that is hard to realize. Once on a
South Texas wolf hunt, we killed eight right in camp—
all thick, stubby fellows, packing sudden death in their
jaws. The Mexicans, who've been raised in company
with them, understand rattlesnakes better than anybody
else and are least afraid of them. Negro labor for clearing
the rattlesnake land is not available, but the Mexicans,
frequently barefooted, wade right in. If, however, a
Mexican has to travel on foot at night, he will usually
sweep a tree branch back and forth over the ground
before him, in order that a rattlesnake, so brushed,
will be prompted to sound off and make himself known.

The wolves we Texans hunt aren't really wolves at
all—just coyotes. There are a few big lobos in the state,
but not many, nothing like the bountiful supply of
coyotes which slink over the southern and western
lands. If you are out hunting without dogs, say stalking
deer, you seldom jump a coyote. But if you look over
your shoulder occasionally, you'll probably see one
crossing your trail behind you, and he'll be the guiltiest
looking fellow you ever saw.

At night the coyotes run in packs and yip and yowl: two very distinct types of vocalizing, one staccato, a constellation of pin points of sound, the other sad and wailing.

Only very seldom will these packs drag down an ailing cow. Sheep and lambs are their dish. Hunters go after them with packs of hounds which run down the coyote (the coyote has more speed but less endurance), bay him, then run in and tear him to pieces—a sport for which I have no stomach.

The trees in this southern and western section are mostly mesquites, a hellish kind of flora that stabs the hand with thorns and refuses to give any shade whatever. And yet to the Westerner, particularly to the Westerner away from home, it is a beloved symbol. Frank Dobie would go cold on two nights to have an open mesquite fire on the third. "It offers a bouquet," he says, "just detectable enough in a well-drawing chimney to gratify alert noses." The thorned branches of the mesquite furnished the first barbed cattle barriers in Texas. Those same thorns have punctured the tires on my car.

The thorns of the cactus compare with those of the mesquite in much the same way that a machine gun compares to a field piece—the cactus punctures you in many more places. This desert plant can live on less water than any vegetable I know. One of its pads thrown on the dry, sun-baked ground will somehow manage to take root there and thrive. Its best trick is to curl into a kind of a cup and draw dew out of the air like a suction pump. When all other cattle-feed fails, the ranchers send men with flame throwers into the prickly pear beds to burn off the thorns. The cattle then eat and will fatten on the cactus. But cattle so trained are apt thereafter to eat the prickly pear, burnt or unburnt, to fill their tongues with so many thorns that the tongue swells out of their mouths. And the animals, unable to eat, die.

Even more Texan are the blue northers that sweep out of the Panhandle under a blue-black sky and sometimes slam the temperature down thirty or forty degrees in a single night.

Too, there is the Mexican road runner, or *paisano*, which in motion looks like a game chicken that has been stretched to extra length. In Texas, out of respect for their taste for snake meat, they are seldom shot.

The javelina, a small wild boar that ranges over our southern ranch lands, will, when wounded, summon his tribe and kill any hunter who does not quickly ascend the nearest tree.

There are also bear and wild cat and mountain lion in Texas. The armadillo, pestiferously, increases every year.

The mustangs, which ran wild over Texas when the first white settlers came, were themselves tough as hickory and not without mettle. It is believed that their origin goes back to the Spanish horses which were brought to this continent by the conquistadores, though by the time the Texans arrived, these horses had, after living a century in a state of nature, bred themselves down to a point where their stature was only three-quarters that of an ordinary horse.

The Texas cow pony is generally bred from quarter-horse stock, which is to say, horses bred to race on a quarter-mile course. Often, for stamina, some mustang blood is introduced, since a cow pony must be tough as well as a quick starter, agile turner, and fast runner. Generally, however, these animals are neither fed corn nor used every day. Each cow hand usually has six horses in the *remuda* and changes every day. Over eighty per cent of the mounts used on United States polo teams are Texas cow ponies.

I have had relations, and not so very long ago, with a Texas bronc, who was not without talent in his line.

I saw him in a pasture one day and liked his looks. He was a big bay, coming four years old. His sun-bleached mane and tail were full of cockleburs, his fetlocks long and shaggy. As he stood in the pasture he wouldn't weigh more than fifty pounds over a thousand. It was early spring, and winter grass had been scarce. The owner wanted only thirty-five dollars for him, and said the horse, though unacquainted with the saddle, was lamb gentle and a great lover of humanity.

I went back to town and picked up a friend of mine who'd been a horse man all his life—range hand in his youth, a livery stable man until cars came. He was addicted to vivid expression.

When we climbed the pasture fence to look at the horse together, Jake turned to me and said, "George, that thin-eared, Roman-nosed son of a bitch will kill you the first time you try to ride him. He'd make good rodeo stock, an' that's all."

Yet, when the owner coaxed the horse into the lot, both the owner and I "forked him," as the saying is, bareback.

So I bought him, to be delivered at the blacksmith shop, where he was to be shod. When I got there the next day, I saw Red, as we called the horse, with his left front foot tied up to his left thigh. That left him three free hoofs. The two hind ones he was using for locomotion; with the front one he was cutting at the blacksmith's head, driving him across the street and up onto a hotel porch.

Finally, however, after more alarums and the application of more ropes, the shoeing was accomplished. Jake took Red to the stable and began plying him with oats and currycomb.

A few days later we put a bridle over Red's halter, forced the bit into his mouth. Next we put a hair blanket, then a saddle, on his back and cinched them down. All this time Red just stood there. Then, untying the halter rope from the post, Jake took a firm hold on the rope and said, "Get on 'im." This I did, and the next thing Jake saw was the tacks in the heels of my shoes as old Red skyrocketed in the air.

I don't believe a horse ever pitched harder or as high. The first jumps were those long, hard, twisting bucks, in which I traveled farther laterally than upward. The next series was straight up and down. I never grabbed for leather. I hadn't that much self-possession. I was utterly ambushed and flabbergasted.

For seven of those terrific, tail-busting jumps I stayed with him. Toward the end he sunfished a little, then hit his Sunday lick. I left the saddle, turned a somersault in the air, and landed elbow down on the hard clay road.

Six weeks later I was able to leave the hospital. And Red had earned for himself a new name. Henceforth we called him Compound Fracture.

> I woke up one morning on the old Chisholm Trail,
> Rope in my hand and a cow by the tail.
>
> Feet in the stirrups and seat in the saddle,
> I hung and rattled with them longhorn cattle.
> —Cowboy Song.

But the greatest of all Texas animals, from the standpoint of Texas' development, the formation of both our fortunes and folkways, were the Longhorn cattle.

"Other states," according to a poem by Berta Hart Nance, "were carved or born; Texas grew from hide and horn."

The old Longhorn has been the subject of so much ridicule, so many people have been at great pains to breed it out of existence, that most people don't realize that without it the development of Texas would probably have been at least a quarter of a century behind its present condition.

Suppose those old-time Texan ranchers had been running fine Hereford stock. How would those Herefords have got to market? On their short, fat, waddling legs? What condition would they have been in after being driven two thousand miles over the ill-watered land? Certainly they would not so well have combated their natural enemies of the range: the mountain lion, the bear, or the coyote packs ogling their newborn calves; not that these considerations are especially pertinent, because the ticks would probably have killed them before these other foes had a chance at them.

Not so with that magnificent old Texian, the Longhorn. The aforementioned inconveniences were right down his street.

What were ticks to his thick hide? As for coyotes, the Longhorns' reply would most certainly have been, "Phooey." As for his ability to trek a couple of thousand miles on foot to the northern markets, that was nothing. What the trail hand was most worried about was keeping his charges from suddenly getting in a hurry and running off and leaving him. Because it was not unusual for a Longhorn steer, in the proper frame of mind, to run all night.

At the very first sign of an impending stampede, and frequently the act preceded the sign, the cow hands would attempt to throw the herd into a mill, that is, get it turning in a tight circle. Unless that could quickly be done, the whole herd was apt to charge off unstoppably through the night, and then it would be "Katy, bar the door."

A Hereford is easy to handle, and we like him because he converts our grasses most profitably into meat, but we Texans don't especially admire his spirit. A

Brahma we are prone to regard as an eccentric, idiotic fool.

But the old Longhorn was spunky as they come. Lots of them just wouldn't bow to the will of mortal man, no matter what he did. They snapped his ropes, gored his horses, and busted his corrals. And it was far less the ruggedness of the country than the disposition of the Longhorn that made his price so much higher tied to a tree than if you bought him F.O.B. wherever you could catch him.

Not only however did his tough old meat sustain our people both as food and profit, his thick hide bound and held us together. Our ropes were plaited out of rawhide. It held our houses together when there were no nails. The harness that drew our persons and property was made of the same material; our furniture— even hats and playing cards—was made out of cowhide.

Undoubtedly, the old Longhorn was the greatest of the Texians. We might still have made it through even without Sam Houston, but the Longhorn, the doughty old aborigine, not only nourished, clothed, and housed us, but set us an example of a way to live.

His time now has come and gone. One day maybe ours will too. If it does, we'll go as he did: with our tails up.

Absolutely our own are the Texas Rangers, and the legend that is theirs. Since 1832 they have fought and quelled whatever the Texas government thought needed quelling. Not all these opponents had to be killed, since most of them knew that if they resisted they would be. One interesting affair in which the Rangers participated occurred at the time the Mexican bandit Cortina, with a band of a hundred men, took possession of the Texas border town of Brownsville, terrorized the citizens, and in the process killed a few. The result was a miniature but business-like war between Cortina and the Rangers who, incidentally, neglected to stop fighting even after they'd driven Cortina's army back into Mexico.

Most of us contemporary Texans remember with pleasure the way in which, in our own life span, the Rangers, working in one-man squads, have cleaned up the toughest towns in Texas (oil boom towns in particular) after every local law enforcement agency had failed. In fact, it was an odd-jobbing ex-Ranger who led the forces that liquidated Clyde Barrow and Bonnie Parker.

A considerably more lively engagement took place in Round Rock in July, 1878, when the Rangers on a squealer's tip went there in search of a man named Bass who'd been making too much money off the railroad.

Sam's ballad begins:

> Sam Bass was born in Indiana, it was his native home;
> And at the age of seventeen young Sam began to roam.
> Sam first came out to Texas, a cowboy for to be. . . .

And that's where he made his mistake. Because Sam was a bad egg from the start and bound to turn outlaw, which he promptly did in the biggest possible way. Starting with stage coaches, he robbed everything that **would** roll and might contain money. In one train robbery, he and his gang netted almost more twenty-dollar gold pieces than they could carry away.

After making himself nationally prominent in respect to robbing rolling stock, it occurred to Sam that banks held money too. And he was in Round Rock with a view to sticking up the local repository, when he locked horns with the Rangers. One contingent of them had, in their eagerness to meet him, ridden sixty-five miles on horseback in one night. Another group with equal zeal had traveled a hundred and ten miles in twenty-three hours.

That hot July afternoon, Bass and his three henchmen: Jackson, Barnes, and the stool pigeon and decoy, Jim Murphy, were camped a little distance out of town. Murphy was sent ahead to reconnoiter. Instead, he ducked into the safety of a stone building.

The other three outlaws rode in a little later and went into a store, ostensibly to buy tobacco, actually to orient themselves into the locale of the impending project. But a Ranger, being informed that the three men were strangers, and thinking he noticed the outline of a gun under one of their coats, walked into the store, touched the bulging coat with his hand, and asked if the man had a gun. The man he'd addressed was Sam Bass.

"Yes," Sam said, and proved it by killing the Ranger at once.

The next Ranger on the scene, a man named Moore, joined the conflict almost immediately and kept on shooting till the store was so full of smoke that the bandits, covered thereby, ran outside. Already two fingers had been shot off of Sam's right hand. By now Ranger Moore had been shot through the left lung, but was still following and firing.

Soon four more Rangers and a citizen or two were participating in the battle. Firing as they ran, the Bass men fought their way to the alley where their horses were tied. But halfway down the alley, a slug tore through Sam's middle. Another burst into and through Barnes's skull. Jackson, the only bandit as yet uninjured, untied Sam's horse and boosted Sam into the saddle. Now Jackson mounted, and, holding Sam in the saddle with his left hand and firing with his right, they dashed across Brushy Creek and made a getaway.

Three miles out of town, when Sam could ride no farther, they hid in a thicket. Jackson, in a kind of fighting frenzy, wanted to stay with Sam and shoot it out with the Rangers.

"No," Sam said, "I'm done for."

He told Jackson to get in his saddle and ride. And, after tying up Sam's wounds as best he could, Jackson mounted and fled.

The next day the Rangers found Sam, half dead in the thicket. They carried him into town, patched him up a little, and gave him the third degree. But it didn't work.

"It's agin' my profession to blow on my pals," Sam said. "If a man knows anything, he ought to die with it in him."

And that's just what he did, the very next day.

Though Sam was in many ways a rat, he was also demonstrably possessed of guts, had died with his boots on refusing to squeal. And everybody in Texas, with the possible exception of the late Rangers' widows and orphaned children, loved him. Nor were the people even partially *simpático* with Murphy, the snitch.

Again the lead-heaving Texas Rangers had got their man, but in getting him they'd made him a martyred Robin Hood as Sam's ballad goes on to tell:

. . . Sam used to coin the money and spent it just as free;
He always drank good whisky, wherever he might be.

Sam left the Collins ranch in the merry month of May
With a herd of Texas cattle, the Black Hills for to see. . . .

On their way back to Texas, they robbed the U. P. train,
And then split up in couples and started out again. . . .

Sam made it back to Texas, all right side up with care—
Rode into the town of Denton, with all his friends to share.
Sam's life was short in Texas—three robberies did he do;
He robbed all the passengers, mail and express cars too. . . .

Sam met his fate at Round Rock, July the twenty-first;
They pierced poor Sam with rifle balls and emptied out his purse.
Poor Sam he is a corpse and six foot under clay;
And Jackson's in the bushes, trying to get away. . . .

But our most peculiar treasure is of course Texians. No more is the concentration very heavy, and that perhaps makes life less hectic and interesting.

Not long ago I asked one of these Texians to make me a pair of boots. But, being, I suppose, a latter-day, decadent Texan, I said I wanted the heels only a couple of inches high rather than three inches. Instead of the customary toes that start out to a very sharp point and, just before the point is reached, are chopped squarely off, I wanted more or less rounded toes.

To save my feelings, the bootmaker did not break off negotiations at once. He gently tried to show me the error of my ways, much as one would treat a mistaken but non-criminal child. Finally, his whole being revolted by the thought of making such a characterless product, he gave up. "I need the business bad," he said, "but be damned if I'll make 'em." I surrendered and told him to make them to suit himself.

When he finished, they were beautiful boots, but too tight.

"Sit down over there," he said, "and we'll start over."

Since he was a poor man and these were twenty-dollar boots, I offered to share his loss on the first pair.

"I guaranteed 'em, didn't I?" he asked me.

"Yes," I said.

"Well I guaranteed 'em. Put your foot up here on my knee."

The second pair was perfect in fit as well as appearance.

One old Texian named Brit Bailey left the following proviso in his will: "Bury me standing up and facing west. I've never looked up to any man yet, and when I'm dead I don't want anybody saying, 'Here lies old Brit Bailey.'"

They buried him standing up, with a jug of whisky at his feet and a rifle by his side.

Not all Texians are male. Once a Texas woman moved to a new town. Her house was next door to the town's leading socialite, to whom the newcomer, a naturally warm and companionable woman, made overtures of friendship. The two got along famously. And when, a week or so later, the socialite gave a reception for local bigwigs, she borrowed heavily of the newcomer's china and silver for the occasion, but neglected to invite the owner to the affair.

After the party, the socialite brought her new neighbor a plate of the party cake to their communal backyard fence. And while the socialite described the high lights of the party to her interested neighbor, she noted that all the chickens in the yard were gathering round. While the newcomer had been listening to the account of the party, she had been quietly crumbling up and raking the cake off the plate onto the ground.

Of course in the old frontier days of Texas, there were more of these valiant souls. My own little town had its quota. For instance, there was one man who used to get drunk on Saturday mornings and start home to the country about noon. He traveled on horseback with a gun across his saddle bow. Most of the other people coming into town for their Saturday trading were still on the road. These our drunk friend forced to turn around and start back. Frequently by the time he was halfway home he was herding a large cavalcade of wagons and buggies down the road in a direction the passengers least wanted to go.

One of my great-uncles, who was of this same thirsty bent, got drunk every time he came to town. Then his friends put him in the buckboard and slapped the horses. Out of town he went, yelling like a Comanche, driving lines trailing on the ground. And the horses always got him home, except for those occasional times when he fell out of the buckboard—which could hardly be charged against the horses.

But while nothing wearing pants could scare this uncle, he was somewhat distrustful of the solar system. During the most recent appearance of Halley's comet, he talked about nothing else for days. Finally, late one night, after sitting out on the porch and disapproving of the comet, he went to bed and at last fell asleep. Just behind and over the headboard of his bed hung a huge family portrait, which chose this of all nights to fall clattering to the floor. My great-uncle woke up running, hickory night shirt flying, yelling at the top of his lungs, "Run for your lives! Halley's comet has fell!"

While present-day Texans have calmed down a little, the Texian strain has by no means disappeared. As a child I knew a man who sometimes lost his temper at the dinner table. On these occasions he caught up the four corners of the tablecloth, dumping dishes and food into the center, and threw the whole thing out the window. Whenever one of his children saw him coming home from the farm, this intelligence was relayed to the other children by the announcement: "Run under the house! Here comes Papa!"

And there is another contemporary one, a "bad man," who feels some responsibility to his reputation. He got drunk in town one Saturday night, did a little hollering, a little cutting, and a little fist fighting. When two officers told him to consider himself under arrest, he declined. They attacked him, using .45 revolvers as clubs—and so used they are dreadful, skull-busting weapons. But despite repeated blows landed by the officers, he whipped them both. They then shot him through the middle, but that didn't help either. Only after they'd shot him again would he let himself be touched by anybody, then not the police. Scheduled to die at once, he rode over to a hospital in a neighboring town and, after a short stay, went back to his cattle and hound dogs and took up his regular duties.

But Texans are not always violent. They are also notorious spenders. I knew one young man who was sent to Chicago by his father in charge of the transportation and sales of a trainload of his father's cattle. In Chicago, the sale consummated, the cash in his pocket, the youth decided to take a look at the town. Four days later he wired his father for railroad fare home.

Texas family life runs the gamut of social position, wealth, and temperament. But I like to feel that the Sheffield family was representative.

There were twelve of the Sheffields. Mr. Sheffield was a small man who seemed to need to be soaked overnight in water, like dried beans, so that his dry little body might swell out into a fresher and less desiccated aspect. He was always riding about the country on an old white horse doing something connected with cattle. But whatever it was, it must not have been lucrative. Mrs. Sheffield had to take in boarders and run an eight-cow dairy.

One morning while Mrs. Sheffield was washing the breakfast dishes, it occurred to her that it was high time the rest of her children were joining the church. Mr. Sheffield had already gone off for the day, so she went to the window and called Cuff, one of the younger boys, who was out under the giant hackberry tree in the back yard trying to rope the cat with a calf rope. She told him to saddle his donkey and go ask Brother Cooper to come over for dinner. She intended to ask Brother Cooper to sprinkle the boys after dinner. These days there were never any more free Sundays. Her boarders and cows required the same fourteen hours of attention on the Sabbath as any other day.

Twice in the past she had led sections of her family into the town's brown frame Methodist church and had them duly baptized, and their names entered upon the church rolls. There had been three candidates in each contingent. But it had been ten years now since the last group had been marshaled to the altar, and there were still four small Sheffields who had not entered the fold.

When Cuff got back, he said Brother Cooper was coming. Mrs. Sheffield made all the boys take their shirts off and scrub themselves and comb their hair. Then she had to hurry to get dinner on the table.

During the meal, between trips to the kitchen, Mrs. Sheffield discussed the baptizing with Brother Cooper. She said she had put a bowl of water on the side table for him to use.

One of the boarders, Lesty McCall, who was the night clerk at the hotel, whispered to Cuff that his mother had forgot the bandage.

"What bandage?" Cuff whispered back.

"For the baptizing."

"Aw . . . "

None of the Sheffield boys had been to church more than once or twice.

"Sure."

Cuff was confused.

"How you mean?" he said.

"Don't you know he's going to baptize you with a pocket knife?"

"Aw . . . I bet you're making that up."

"I guess you don't remember what happened to that Levy kid when the doctor baptized him?"

Cuff was turning pale.

"Jews have the doctor," Lesty added. "Methodists just have the preacher."

"It does seem a shame," Mrs. Sheffield said, bringing in a chocolate pie, "that I let them boys get this big without getting baptized."

"I've always thought it was better to tend to that while they were young," Lesty said.

"That's right, Brother McCall," Brother Cooper said.

Brother Cooper was not tall but he weighed more than two hundred pounds. He could not sit close to the table on account of his stomach.

"No'm," Cuff said, when his mother passed the pie around.

As soon as all the boarders were gone, Mrs. Sheffield said, "All right, you boys let Brother Cooper baptize you. He's going to have to excuse me because I got to get the kitchen cleaned up before milking time."

Mrs. Sheffield went into the kitchen to put her dishwater on the stove.

The minute she was out of sight, Cuff, white in the face, yelled, "Run! He's gonna cut us like we was Jews or yearlings!"

In the kitchen Mrs. Sheffield heard chairs falling and bare feet running. Before she could get into the dining room, she saw through the window that the boys were scrambling up the big hackberry tree in the back yard. Then, still standing at the window, she heard them drop one by one from the limb of the tree to the top of the house, and Dick, the youngest boy, screaming in frightened delight, "Ole Fatty ain't gonna catch us, is he?"

Mrs. Sheffield wiped her hands on her apron and went outside to try to get them down.

8. What Texans Do for Fun

*L*IKE most everybody else, Texans like to talk, and do a lot of it. In my town for instance the social life, in the sense of even semi-formal parties, is anything but strenuous. Most people who want to entertain invite several couples, build a fire in their backyard barbecue pit, open a bottle of whisky, and barbecue a few steaks. In some communities, the fish-fry is substituted for the barbecue. At Georgetown, for example, no other type of refreshment enjoys the almost drooling approbation with which its citizens regard a dishpan full of fried suckers, freshly netted from the San Gabriel River. But principally we just visit around, drop in on friends (without appointment) and leave as soon as we've stopped having a good time.

During the day the men visit over coffee cups or Coca-Colas, talk business and crops and local gossip, while the women do most of their daytime visiting over the telephone. At this pastime, the country women hold the advantage, because theirs are party-line phones, which afford three- or four-way conversations, to say nothing of mild opportunities for eavesdropping. Mild, because your neighbors know you're listening, and won't tell much of what they don't want you to hear. The town women also have bridge parties and similar passive measures to combat the empty hours.

In our cities there are downtown clubs for the business-men, as well as country clubs. In the small towns, there of course are no men's clubs beyond a scattering of Rotary and Kiwanis groups. Furthermore, most of the small-town lodge chapters have long since taken the count. They couldn't compete with the radio and movies and the numerous places where men can gather and talk at night without paying dues.

In our town the principal hang-outs are the cafes, the confectioneries, the domino parlor, and Mr. B. Ashby's garage. At the garage in the winter a fat stove stoked with lignite coal keeps the big, comfortably roomy and unkempt office cozy and warm. On summer evenings the half-dozen chairs and several sturdy ammunition boxes (Mr. B. also sells ammunition) are set out in front of the garage where the south wind blows.

Here on summer nights we discuss fishing and politics. In the winter, hunting and politics. Too, there is talk of what happened in the not so distant past in our town. Someone may mention the time my Great-Uncle John Perry wrote a drenchingly sentimental story for one of the local papers. It was called *A Romance of the Old San Gabriel.* A week later, John ("K. Lamity") Bonner came back in the competing paper with a parody entitled *Paw Paw Pete,* or *The Fatal Mess of Chitterlings.*

Then, almost inevitably, someone will recall the delicate yet expressive phrase coined by the same Bonner in his weekly *Harpoon.* He was attacking certain politicians for their galling slowness, inaction, inefficiency, and general sloth. Admonished K. Lamity: "If you're not going to answer nature's call, please vacate the crockery."

Or we may discuss one of the almost legendary local heroes. He drank cisterns full of whisky and fought anything that would make a track. Rumors that he was dying from injuries received in his various fights became first commonplace, then boring. We had seen him returning from conflict, his own entrails in his arms, and had seen him get sewed up and recover. He was always too drunk to die. Finally, however, some pallid, unworthy illness laid him low. His instructions for the disposition of his remains were: "Just pour me back in the bottle."

During these pleasant evenings at Mr. B.'s, most of the fishing talk is catfish talk. Because catfish fishing is a poor man's sport, and most of us are in varying degrees poor. To go catfishing, all that's needed is fifteen cents' worth of hooks and a quarter's worth of line. This outfit will last all summer. It is also well to have a minnow seine and a minnow bucket, but usually these last-named items are borrowed and not necessarily returned. The same applies to rowboats.

Most people like catfishing because it frequently amounts to a kind of party with three or four fishermen present. When the lines are baited, tied to a willow twig and the weighted end thrown into the water, there is an hour or two to kill between each tour of inspection. And this, with several men around a camp fire (catfishing is generally done at night) is not hard to do. Perhaps there are a few fish to fry, a bottle of something to drink, a little stud poker to play. And next to football, I suspect catfishing is the most popular Texas sport.

Football of course touches everybody. Every high school has its team, and each town takes its football seriously. And all Texas is proud of its college teams. The old issue of whether college football players should or should not be subsidized is, so far as Texas is concerned, dead. Most any Texas college will take care of a good football prospect's tuition, and a majority will also furnish board and lodging. But to a really brilliant Texas high school football star, such limited inducements are apt to appear humdrum. He is then promised an attractive summer vacation job in the firm of some flush alumnus. That failing, a fancy permanent job, at a junior executive's salary, is promised to him as soon as he shall have graduated.

But graduation is four years hence. Perhaps a sinecure of some kind can be found for him. Sometimes there is more than one mouth to feed. For example, on the squad of the great University of Texas team of 1941, there were nine married men, two with babies—which no doubt periodically needed a new pair of shoes. For building this team and for an over-all period of service of ten years, Coach Bible will receive the satisfying total of $150,000.

Yet while there is a special tendency toward flamboyance, or razzle-dazzle, as the sporting press prefers to call it, in Texas football, that sport is, after all, All American.

Texas deer hunting is a different matter. There just aren't as many deer in other places. And though in Texas they damage crops, hunting rights will usually bring the rancher considerably more revenue than the damage incurred. As a general thing the rancher counts on that source of revenue to pay his taxes.

Many of our oil *nouveaux riches* divert themselves with ranches, fancy fishing and hunting preserves, and gambling for spectacular stakes.

The Old Line country club people, like those elsewhere, derive a lot of pleasure from being so affiliated. The men play golf, and their ladies eat chicken salad and potato chips on the club veranda. Here bridge is the staple game, just as dominoes is in the small towns.

The small-town domino parlors are cool, comfortably dirty places, the floor covered with the markings of other seasons' ambeer, the air carrying a flavorsome load of ripe profanity and witticism.

The poor man's night clubs are the honky-tonks, the roadside beer parlors and whisky arenas that clutter the outskirts of our towns, and in which, gallon for gallon, more blood has been shed than ever was lost at the Alamo. It is such places as these that an inebriated Texan of an active disposition may elect to wreck. And once that project has been begun, a certain mass abandonment of decorum is likely to manifest itself, the repercussions of which may extend to several hospitals and first-aid stations as well to the justice of the peace court the following morning.

One of the most vicious aspects of the honky-tonk is to be found not in what it is (and to be sure it is in itself disgusting and degrading), but in the really luminous and wonderful folk entertainments it tends somewhat to displace, especially the country house dances, where there always were enough fist fights and associated diversions to satisfy the requirements of normal people. I remember in particular those given by an extremely hospitable country man who was a farmer by vocation, and by avocation now a bootlegger, now a Holiness preacher, according to his mood at the time. When his house was so jampacked with dancers that there was room for no more, yet still more dancers were arriving, the fiddlers and *gui*-tar pickers were boosted to the rafters. Precariously perched on these cross members, the leader then struck up "Chicken in the Bread Pan" or another and equally lively selection, and away the dancers went—including the two or three additional couples this elevation of the orchestra had made room for.

Soon the rhythmic stomp of the dancers, for the only direction in which they could move was perpendicular, set the old house first to pulsating, then dangerously to rocking. And if any of the more cautious spirits suggested thinning out the crowd, the host, intoxicated by, among other things, the sight of so many of his guests having a good time, yelled, "Just keep on a-dancin', folks. Dance er to the ground!"

Here of course lack of space made "round" dances, as opposed to square dances, obligatory. Under less crowded circumstances the latter were frequently practiced and were more fun. The loping, prancing step, the ringing cries of the caller: "Swing your partners to and fro. Step out now and do a *do si do!*"—all these things seemed to engender a merriment that round dancing never could. These dancing parties and play-parties, sometimes called Josie parties, are the wholesome institutions the honky-tonk threatens.

Even more widespread pleasure was, until a few years ago, derived by the country people from their churches. But some awful thing, some cold intrusion, an ugly half-baked sophistication, has begun to put a blight on the country church and its wonderful associated enterprises such as the lively, deeply felt and wholly diverting feuds that grew out of church politics, and the box suppers by which church funds were raised. At these functions a man's pride would not permit him to be outbid for the lunch box prepared by the lady of his choice, for with ownership of the box went the privilege of dining with her who had prepared it. Then there were the splendid camp meetings and revivals held in the summer beneath a brush-arbor tabernacle— where souls were saved and re-saved, and where the spirit of festival, of re-acquaintance and long visits with old friends, was the order of the day.

Too there were amusing incidents. Most families brought their dogs. And generally some bad boys affixed a pin to the nose of one of those friendly animals —usually just before the beginning of services.

Then as the dogs wandered about the tabernacle and greeted each other according to canine etiquette, all those saluted by this armed carnivore set up mysterious howls until finally at the very sight of him the other dogs yelped, tucked their tails, and flew pell-mell through the crowd.

But while these fine old institutions are now in abeyance, others that are also fine persevere.

There are still community singings. Here the best voices in the community practice throughout the year for the all-important district competition, the singing convention, at which thousands will drench themselves in the joys of old-time songs—and the thrill of rich, strong, country voices, practiced to perfection, bearing down on "That Old Time Religion" for the honor and glory of their community, be it Dime Box, Frog Jaw, or Sipe Springs.

Nor will the glories of these moments ever be lost.

Among other able Boswells (such as the Lomaxes, *père et fils*) of the folk beauties of this land, there is a merry historian named Bill Owens from A. and M. College, who is always Johnny-on-the-spot with his recording machine.

If there are any of the old songs that the singers don't know, he'll teach them to the singers. If it's an archaic dance step they want demonstrated, all Bill wants is room. Drawing upon an unbelievable mental catalogue of such items, he will step out and make the splinters fly.

In his record collection there are wonderful experiences for the listener not elsewhere to be found. Such items as a Negro woman singing a song she composed called "Heaven's Radio" in which the words are the expression of a simple mind, so simple as *almost* to cause the listener to laugh before the music, the exquisite expression of the reverence and humility and inner beauty of a great artist's soul, catches and thrills and humbles the listener—leaves him buffeted by the taxing experience of almost blinding beauty.

Bill Owens knows all these folk singers, the frequently illiterate poets and minstrels. He knows the Grey Ghost of Navasota, the starving, talented balladist who composed "De Hitler Blues," which was played and publicized all over the world—and yet by his music the Ghost has never earned the price of a two-bit bottle of paregoric.

There is General Washington (another of Bill's colored friends) who is a principal singer in a quartet known as "The Uplifted Fo'." But the General's musical interests extend further than that. "We got a band," he says, "right here in the family. Sister Carrie, she plays the piano. Me and my son, the Colonel, we sing. Brother John plays a instru*ment* that is known as the violin. My other brother, he beats on the wall with a broom."

But most exclusively Texan of all these various entertainments, and it is by no means entirely exclusive, is the rodeo. The great relish with which it is attended and participated in by Texans is but further evidence of the fact that ranching in most Texan minds is more of a pleasure than a business. For what, after all, is a rodeo besides certain selected workaday phases of ranching—breaking wild horses, roping cattle, bull-dogging steers that must be thrown in order to be doctored for cuts? Its kinship with ranching, its danger and brilliant demonstrations of skill are what make the rodeo good box-office in Texas.

Besides, there is usually a barbecue in conjunction, a few slaughtered beeves and sheep and pigs roasting on an open fire, being mopped with "sop" by a colored man.

A less well known fact is that Texas is a great fox-hunting state. We haven't got any red coats and wouldn't know a tally-ho from a grommet, yet on any clear, still night the Texas woods will contain hundreds of fox hunters.

These men will be sitting around fires, hunting by ear, listening to the distant hounds, knowing by the bawling of the dogs precisely what is going on, visualizing every detail, knowing which dog is distinguishing himself and which isn't. There is little talk beyond an occasional whisper, as these quiet men sit still, looking into the fire with glazed eyes, experiencing the emotions of the hunt.

Unlike certain more effete localities, we still have and enjoy railroad excursions down here. It is true that before the advent of the automobile, the excursion was in even greater vogue. Huge Sunday School picnics were organized to take advantage of low-rate trips. But a still greater fad among the adolescent male passengers was that of "hopping" the train after it had started. It was just one of the things that were done. A spirited boy would no more board or debark from a stationary train than he would be caught wearing a bonnet. An uncle of mine, who in his boyhood was an absolute fiend on the subject of train hopping and showing off generally, spent one whole excursion-picnic-Sunday hiding in the men's toilet of an empty excursion train because, on hopping off the train as it neared its destination, he had misjudged his distance, gone sailing belly-down across the gravelly station yard, and scrubbed the whole front out of his Sunday suit.

Present-day excursion trains usually run to the Mexican border towns. During Prohibition, of course, we made the trip chiefly to get a change from the eternal corn whisky that was corroding our insides. Here, for six bits, you could get a bottle of pretty good Mexican rum. One of these would see you through the bullfight that afternoon, four or five more through the entire excursion.

The crowded train on its homeward journey, loaded to the guards with poor folks and cheap liquor, was usually characterized by crap games in the baggage car, fist fights in the aisles, and veritable windrows of those less temperate souls who had passed out cold.

For some reason I loved those uncomfortable trips. I loved the cool Cadillac Bar in Nuevo Laredo in the hours before the bullfight, its walls plastered with bright, brave, swirling posters of the imminent *corrida*, people eating blue quail on toast and naïvely complaining that it was tough, whole squads of bartenders shaking cocktails in the same rhythm.

Here was the town where the celebrated Sidney Franklin was gored, where Gaona had done his stuff, where the great Balderas was fighting bravely, talentedly, with great belief in the importance and beauty of his job.

Other excursions went to Eagle Pass. Across the river from Eagle Pass lies Piedras Negras, with its great abundance of saloons, cabarets, whorehouses, and the great red bull ring.

Here one morning I went with Pépé Ortiz when he sized up and drew for the bulls he was to fight that day. And the one he principally did not want to get, he got. The bull's horns were long and his eyes were bad. The flick of the cape would never register on him. Instead he would smell for his man. And while, with the cape, a fighter can suggest to the bull that the fighter is located where he isn't, it is considerably more difficult to stand on one spot and smell as if you were somewhere else.

When the fight started that afternoon, the vaunted understanding of the fine points by the *aficionados* was strangely lacking. Ortiz was making a mess of the fight, and they didn't care why. Immediately then, the fact that he was being humiliated by a blind bull, which a moment or so later would probably kill him, was further complicated by the hail of beer bottles which kept flying at his head. But by relying strongly on the principle of retreat, he managed to live through this very sordid affair.

My own despondence was a little later repaired at the restaurant of Felipe Chong with a dish of black little Mexican *aguacates* and a platter of *cabrito* (roast breast of baby goat), a dish that is truly sublime.

Of course politics is one of our greatest sources of entertainment, but as in most other communities *l'amour* develops more interest than anything else. But since that is a private matter, perhaps silence best behooves us. For if a Texan is going to kill you, he'd rather do it because of a woman than most anything else, including fence cutting. For a long time we were known as the womanless republic. A wife was hard to get, and once you got her you prized her, and shot the top of anybody's head off who looked crossways at her—a procedure that Texas juries have consistently applauded. So let us abandon that explosive topic and pass on to a consideration of Texas' stomach-busting vittles.

9. Bill O' Fare

$\mathcal{I}$T is said that in the frontier days the frying pan killed more Anglo-Americans than did the Indians. But that is because the frying pan had no competition from the present-day small Texas town cafe plate lunch. Otherwise the honors would have been differently distributed.

Like most people I like to eat. I have a splendid appetite and the digestion of a billy goat, but when I am confronted by one of those small town blue plates, I've met my match.

Maybe those things exist in, and harass the citizens of, other states. For some reason I've never run across them. In any case they can't be any worse than the ones we have in Texas.

"Will you have the roast beef or the roast pork or the fried steak?" If you take either of the first two items, they will, through some malignant magic, have been turned a repulsive light grey color and have both the flavor and texture of a thrice-boiled tennis shoe. The fried steak is a tough, greasy mess that only the most famished hound could relish. In addition to these *pièces de résistance formidables*, you get a dollop of boiled navy beans, a cud of greasy turnip greens, and maybe a sliver of sweet potato. For dessert there is a piece of pie with which you would hesitate to strike your most hated enemy.

That is Texas food at its most widespread worst. Actually we haven't any indigenous cuisine outside of a few short-order gastronomic horrors. Like all Texans I'm proud of the state and wish that in this connection there was something favorable to say. If there is, I don't know what it is.

Mind you, we do not go without the delicacies or the cooking techniques of the rest of the nation. Our housewives take the women's magazines and know how to do a double handstand with such standardized items as Jello and Kraft dinner. But essentially, judging by our public eateries, we are still a frying-pan state.

Most of us don't even know a decent piece of beef when we see it. We have little enough discrimination to prefer veal. The cow people know better. Pat Boyt says that during his boyhood the cowboys would often break an old cow's leg, in order to have an excuse to kill it for beef, since chuckwagon cooks preferred to cope with veal. Most of our housewives have the same unfortunate tendency.

It is true that there are a few distinguished places to

eat in Texas. Among them are Kelly's Steak House in Houston, a Negro barbecue stand called Black Boy's near Hempstead, San Jacinto Inn near Houston, Harry Lewis's root beer stand in Waco (don't laugh—Duncan Hines thinks so, too), and a few others. To my notion, the *Carta Blanca* serves the best Mexican food in San Antonio. Most of the big hotels have the kind of food you'd expect: adequate, and that's about all.

In Southeast Texas, of course, the French influence is felt. People do interesting things with seafood and rice, but not as well as it is done in New Orleans.

A few of our rural citizens still make their own ash hominy in their own wash pots, and few dishes have greater character or, despite its simplicity, more subtle implications of flavor.

The principal "sweetenin'" of many of us Texans is blackstrap molasses, which is made not of sugar cane, but of sorghum cane, which if left to the uses God meant for it, would be eaten by some undiscriminating mule with no more than a few occasional grimaces.

If you like tamales and don't mind taking the trouble to make them, you'd still better not try. In the first place, you'd have to grind your own meal Mexican fashion, from soft, well-soaked corn, instead of using ordinary meal which is ground from dry corn. And in the second place, an unpracticed hand will probably make a mess of the tamales anyway, since not only must you have patience, experience, and a supply of corn shucks for wrappings, but a great deal of troublesome steaming is necessary. The best place for ordinary mortals to get tamales is out of a can, unless there is some wayside vendor at hand. I never saw a tamale peddler in my life who manifested the slightest interest in sanitation, but I also don't remember ever buying any of their wares (invariably out of a ten-gallon lard can) that weren't, for all their skimping on the meat content, tasty and good. The best ones, to my taste, are made not from beef or chicken, but from hog's heads.

The *taco* (Mexican hamburger: a little smear of ground meat, several squirts of liquid fire, and some chopped-up lettuce and tomatoes all wadded into a fried *tortilla*) is easily enough made if you've got the *tortillas*. An *enchilada*, which most of us Texans like better, is a heartier item, made by rolling a *tortilla* around a gob of *chile con carne*, chopped raw onion, and grated cheese.

But the best and simplest of all the Tex-Mex concoctions is a platter of frijole beans that have first been endlessly boiled, then mashed and fried.

The Mexican notion of how to stuff a bell pepper revolves chiefly around the use of a lot of raisins, and that recipe they can have back. For that matter, unless you keep a Mexican cook under constant surveillance, he will put sugar in everything, and then, idiot-like, expect to be commended.

The Mexicans are also fond of the fruit of the cactus, which I find not worth the trouble it takes to swallow the stuff. This same fruit is also crystallized and sold on most Texas trains on the implied basis that it's edible.

The best thing in most small-town restaurants is the pot of *chile con carne* they keep simmering on the back of the stove. It will blitz your digestion, but it does make a kind of sense while you're eating it.

Also good is Texas barbecue (the word deriving from the French, I'm inclined to believe, meaning from beard to tail because originally whole animals were cooked this way). At a huge public gathering, say a rodeo, it is apt to be inedible. But from the roadside stands of the regular practitioners it will probably be succulent and consoling—if, that is, you like highly seasoned food. If you wonder what's contained in the sauce that is periodically sopped over the roasting meat, its major ingredients are vinegar, cooking oil, salt and black pepper, though every cook adds fillips all his own.

In order to make the cheap cuts of low-quality, grass-fed cattle tender, many barbecue cooks first boil the meat for an hour or so. The fact that most of the natural flavor is thereby dissipated is, they feel, unimportant, since the sauce can be made so strong that nothing else can be tasted anyway.

In Texas we barbecue anything that will hold still: beef, pork, mutton, chicken, wild fowl, fish, even venison. And the least well suited to this type of cooking is beef, since by the time it is done it is frequently bone-dry.

One of our springtime dishes is wild poke greens. By many it is considered a spring tonic. But unless well parboiled and re-cooked in different water, it is apt to be explosively cathartic.

As a matter of fact, most Texas poor folks were reared on boiled collards, boiled turnip greens, dried beans or peas, and the salt pork cooked therewith. That, and cornbread and molasses.

Just as all Negro songs are either religious in character or are "sinful songs," cornbread is of two unequivocal genres. The cornbread that most of the United States eats, my parents called "egg bread." The regular, and the better kind, is composed simply of scalded corn-meal and a little salt. After being allowed to sit long enough for the meal grains to swell, it is then fried on a griddle and is, to my taste, wonderful.

In the western part of the state there is a favorite stew known, if I may be pardoned for accurate reporting, by the name of "son of a bitch." Like most stews it is composed chiefly of the kitchen residuum, but usually the basic ingredients are corn, beans, onions, and the late genitals of an ex-bull—a dish chiefly in evidence in early spring and late fall, which are the cutting seasons.

But where Texas cooking comes furthest to the fore is in the preparation of the humble hamburger. And there is as much difference between a Texas hamburger and one made in the East as there is between Sam Houston and Calvin Coolidge.

In the East a hamburger means a pat of grilled meat in a naked bun. In Texas it means a short-order tantrum, and the sky's the limit. In this state when you're asked if you want a hamburger "with everything on it," you'd better take the trouble to ask what "everything" means.

All of which would seem to me to be but further proof that we are a genuinely hardy people, who have been tough enough to triumph, not only over the Indians, the Mexicans, and the politicians, but also over the skillet.

10. Water, Sweet and Salty

$\mathcal{P}$ERHAPS no other state is as water-conscious as Texas. Along the upper eastern coast there's several times too much. Out west there's many times too little. In the east we spend millions on drainage ditches; in the west we spend millions on dams. In all, we irrigate between a half and three quarters of a million acres of land—and that takes a lot of water. It is only a shortage of water in Texas' western areas that has caused them to remain America's greatest land frontier.

The biggest natural lake in Texas is the Caddo, of some seventy thousand acres, on the Texas-Louisiana line. Most big Texas lakes are artificial ones built on our rivers. On the Colorado, for example, the Lower Colorado River Authority has strewn the valley with forty-five million dollars' worth of dams, which are supposed to control floods and impound water for generating electricity.

On the Brazos, which sweeps through Central Texas, lies Waco, home of Baptist Baylor University, a wholesaling city of 55,000, which can use the financial shot in the arm that is being given to it by the new military aviation installations located there.

In the middle distance between Waco and the sea, the Brazos is edged by plantations which are very Old South in every sense. Evidently the Spaniards were pretty thirsty when they bumped into the Brazos for the first time. For, referring to its two separate upper branches, they enthusiastically named it *Los Dos Brazos de Dios:* The Two Arms of God. The Brazos is, incidentally, a very comfortable old river, seldom very clear, and containing some wondrous catfish.

The Red River, which demarcates much of Texas' northern boundary, is being dammed by a fifty-million-dollar power and flood control project. This system will flood 95,000 acres of land—26,000 of which lie in Oklahoma, and may result in renewed armed conflict between Texas and her northern step-sister. (When Oklahoma's Governor Alfalfa Bill Murray got mad at Texas over an interstate highway bridge, he promptly began mobilizing and marching the state militia and closing roads.)

But the most useful Texas river—at least, one side of it belongs to Texas—is the Rio Grande, which meanders fifteen hundred winding miles along Texas' southwest border, nourishing Texas' appallingly fruitful Lower Rio Grande Valley. Here, at all seasons of the year, vegetables and citrus fruit grow like mad. The grass in the yards in front of the houses may be brown and brittle, but across the fences the lettuce patches and orange groves will be a violent, almost giddy green.

A dozen years ago the Valley was still in a state of turbulence and growth—land prices, particularly if a few grapefruit seedlings grew out of the ground, ran to two thousand dollars an acre, and from there, of course, to the bankruptcy courts.

When the boom was on in the Valley, no higher powered promoters were elsewhere to be found. Special trainloads of prospective clients ripped across Texas from the Middle West several times a week. It is said that on one of these excursions, as the train approached an area which was inundated with the muddy overflow from rampaging creeks, the quick-witted promoter, to keep his charges from seeing this disheartening sight, called upon them all to kneel in the aisle and give thanks to God for the blessed opportunity He had thrown their way.

Down on their knees sank those about to be shorn. And the prayer, of no doubt particular thankfulness, was stretched by the promotor from dry land to dry land.

In any case, to emerge from the South Texas Brasada onto this unlikely-seeming, hundred-mile-long Eden is a strange and somehow unsettling experience. One moment the traveler is in the dry, mesquite-covered semi-desert—the next moment in a blooming grove. The line of demarcation from the domain of the rattlesnakes to that of the moccasins is usually only two or three feet wide.

But stranger yet is the prompt change in the various collateral manifestations of these two adjacent civilizations. In one the land is under the sway of the King *vaqueros*, in the other under that of expatriated Middle Westerners.

And while the visitor is impressed by obvious and widespread wealth, there is also something pretty creepy about the whole place. It works, but you get the feeling that it all came as a pretty big surprise to God.

Of course there is a reasonably continuous contest between these new Texans and the Mexicans to see who can pump the most water out of the limited supply afforded by the Rio Grande. However, it is felt by persons acquainted with this situation that our side is not being cheated out of its riparian "rights."

Since all the land in this area will grow crops the year around, it's only the limitation of available water that keeps the very cheap dry land from being worth as much as the three- or four-hundred-dollar-an-acre irrigated land just across the fence.

It is this almost inestimable value of water that has filled so many cattlemen with disgust when their drilling operations have supplied them with oil instead of water.

In this land of newcomers, it is easy to look across a field where men are plowing and determine whether the plowman be an Old Line Texan or a transplanted Middle Westerner. If the farmer follows the plow, he's probably from Minnesota. But if the plowman has saddled one of the plow horses and is riding it as he plows, that farmer is not far from his place of birth.

Our rivers are important to us not only as means of irrigation, but also as transportation. Seagoing vessels come up the Sabine to Orange, up the Neches to Port Arthur and Beaumont. And since Houston had such good luck bringing the ocean fifty miles inland to its door, the city of Dallas and a certain Commodore Hatfield, a fabulous figure of the Trinity River, are trying to dredge the Trinity so that ships may proceed from tidewater to far inland Dallas.

For all our vast interior land masses, Texans are not entirely without a feeling for the sea or without a certain maritime tradition. As this is written, Chester Nimitz, a Texas man, is running the fleet at Hawaii. And at one time we Texans owned and operated our own navy. That was during the Texas Revolution. Four small vessels, the *Invincible*, the *Brutus* (there was irony in the name of this one), the *Independence*, and the *Liberty*, harassed Mexican commerce and made the attempted Mexican blockade of Texas ports more or less ineffective.

This fleet was under the command of Commodore E. W. Moore, formerly of the United States Navy. Commodore Moore attacked and captured Tabasco and Yucatán and several other coastal towns. But unfortunately the Navy got enjoying itself so hugely that it simply flaunted Sam Houston's orders to cease and desist grabbing booty for itself.

Finally, in disgust, Sam said the Navy was just a

bunch of pirates and gave the whole works to the United States Government, which incorporated the vessels into its own Navy.

But there is really no use pretending that our maritime talents were our forte. They weren't. A Texian's seat belonged in a saddle, and once he got it there, he was a hard man to beat.

In fact, we fought one of our most effective naval engagements during the Texas Revolution on horseback.

It happened when a flotilla of the Mexican Navy charged into Copano Bay, swept all before it, and dominated the scene with great majesty—until the tide went out, grounding the Mexican vessels.

At that point, seeing the Mexicans were immobilized, the Texans mounted and attacked, their horses now swimming, now touching the bay floor, being so guided that they never came in range of the stationary cannon of the Mexican ships, which were promptly stormed and taken.

At least that's what one of the history books says. I don't guarantee the authenticity of this incident, but it seems a plausible, and is an entertaining, idea.

11. How to Talk Texas

WHEN a land becomes over-civilized, its language is apt to lose much of the quality of fruity surprise that has characterized it during the less effete periods. Already in Texas the Negroes are emerging as our grand champions in the matter of original expression.

Once I asked a Negro man why he and his co-worker had not accomplished more work. "Cause we both wasn't workin' hard," he said. "I done my part, but Jeris, he ratted on the job. An when I tried to get 'im to go on an' do right, he said I didn't have no *compeltry* over him."

Manifestly such diction is fostered by the Negro's hunger to be understood. It is his poverty of grammatically-ready-made expression patterns and his extremely limited vocabulary that force upon him this rich inventiveness of ignorance.

When a Negro acts superior to his fellows, he is accused of "acting bigly." Our cook invites callers whom she meets at the door to "rest their hats and coats." When the Negro's ordinarily precarious financial condition grows even worse, he's apt to refer to that condition as "whettin' on the point," or say that he is "unfinancial." One who is determined to make a living claims, "I'm gonna keep my skillet greasy." In the sawmill communities a mean Negro is a "tush hog nigger." (Most long-tusked hogs are fighting hogs.)

Many of the most beautiful of these Negroisms have been recorded in fiction by Roark Bradford, across the border in Louisiana, where a wife of doubtful allegiance is known as "a frivolin' woman," and where a Negro's prestige is much affected by his ability to "talk good experience" in church.

Yet in a land which Jim Ferguson, when at outs with the state university, accused of "having gone hog wild over higher education," many splendid old Texasisms still prevail.

Some Texans came here without enough clothes "to dust a fiddle" through mud "that would bog a snake." If one were surprised at what he found, "his eyes bugged out to where you could rope 'em with a grapevine."

If you were visiting in a Texas home and a transient jackass entered the living room, ate all the flowers out of the vases, and then quietly departed, your host, after a moment of utter bewilderment, might remark, "Well, that *does* take the rag off the bush."

In the old days when a boastful cowboy moved to a new community and wanted to give himself an all-inclusive recommendation, he would, in less delicate terms, declare that he was: a fornicator, a fighter, a wild horse rider, and right smart of a windmill fixer. This expression is with us yet.

To have intimidated another person is to have him "buffaloed" or "tee-roned." To bring him to taw: to make him "come up to the lick log." Eagerness is frequently expressed by the word "horsing."

Oil has introduced many new words into our diction. To try to get information from someone is an attempt to "swab" him. A seismograph crew is a "shootin' crew"; its less specialized members are "ground stompers." An oil field trucker's assistant is otherwise noted as a "swamper."

Ranching terms that have come into the language are legion. A "maverick" is a free and rambunctious soul. It got its meaning from a herd of cattle which a man named Maverick (ancestor of Maury) had put on an island pasture, but which swam ashore and roamed over the countryside to be captured and branded by whoever could turn the trick. Ribbing, or a series of embarrassing jokes at a person's expense, is called "rawhiding" from the old days when a newcomer in a cow camp was sometimes hazed with a pair of rawhide chaps.

If a man falls in a creek, his companion may report that he was soaked "from his head to his hocks." A vacuum is said to be "empty as a sheep-herder's head."

Anything particularly lively is "frisky as a cutting horse." When joy is unconfined, "the bridle's off!"

We frequently refer to our children not as being, say, six years old, but as "coming seven." A foolish person we sometimes call "a hollow horn." Or we may say that he is "loco," because a horse that eats the loco weed behaves idiotically. A corpulent Texienne may be said to be "packin' plenty tallow."

An unattached Texan threatened by local difficulties may remark that he's not thereby terribly inconvenienced, that all he has to do before going elsewhere is to "wet on the fire and call the dogs." If he leaves in a particular hurry, his neighbors may remark, "That fellow really lit a shuck," or "he was mortally toppin' cotton."

For many of our local expressions derive from our close association with cotton. If a man is seen doing something in great haste, we say that he was "really ginnin'." Cotton lore blends with oil lore in the appellation of a small-time or "boll-weevil drilling rig." "Bumblebee cotton" is cotton so feeble and low to the ground that a bumblebee can lie on its back and kick the locks out of the bolls.

From the old days of broad, shrubless plains and few privies, we frequently, if less delicately, refer to times of great prosperity as those in which we were defecating "in high cotton." From this same derivation comes the expression, "In distance, there's decency."

The principal outside influence on our language is, of course, that of the Mexican. Many people who wouldn't know an *estancia* from a goose-liver sandwich often remark that it is time to "*vamos por la casa,*" which is supposed to be Spanish for "I must go home." The word "vamoose" derives directly therefrom. We call our jails "the calaboose" from the Spanish *calabozo* or "hoosegow" from *juzgado.*

We, like the Mexicans, refer to men as "*hombres,*" only we call it "umbry." Our famous lariats derive from the Spanish *la riata.* The word "ranch" itself comes from the Mexican word *rancho.* Anything that is free we call a "*pilone,*" which is what the Mexicans call the little free sack of candy our border grocers still give a Mexican family which has bought a substantial order of groceries.

For a superlative action as, say, in the case of playing a violin, we remark, "He sawed that fiddle to a who laid the chunk." Somewhat anomalously we say of a friend who failed to return that "he came up missing."

Our deepest backwoods we refer to as a place where the owls have non-platonic relations with the chickens and where the same lax condition exists between the coyotes and the sheep dogs. Or we may say of a portion of West Texas, "a crow has to carry his own rations when he flies over it." The Pecos River has enough alkali in it "to give a kildee the diarrhea just to cross it."

To express choice, we say, "If I had my druthers, I'd druther do so and so." A person who goes to all the parties is "gallivantin'." A Negro or poor white shanty is a "shotgun shack" or a "sharpshooter."

In the face of appalling news we sometimes remark, "I'll be a sawed-off scissor bill." A Texan faced with insuperable difficulties sometimes declares, "I wish I'd been born a gal baby," or that he wishes a panther had caught him when he was young, or "I've got as much chance as a stump-tailed bull in fly time."

When a Texan is assigned some job he believes impossible but which he is yet willing to take a fling at, he'll reply, "Well, like a steer, I can try."

When conditions generally are bad, we say, "They said it would be hell when it was this-a-way, and it's this-a-way now."

In East Texas we invite guests over by saying, "Come sit on my porch and chew cane." For an honored guest we "put the big pot in the little one, fry the skillet and throw the handle away."

We've "got our kettle on" for our enemies, so that we can scald him at our convenience. If we shoot him, we "blow a window in him," or "ventilate him."

A tasty dish is "larrupin'," which could have come from the use of the same word meaning a "beating," thus developing a connotation of superiority.

My father always referred to a large number or quantity of anything as a "passel." A lightning action is said to have been committed "before God got the news." A man who's done nothing "hasn't so much as stirred a stump."

Instead of throwing, we "chunk" things. We don't husk corn; we "shuck" it. Our acorn crop is a "mass" or "mast" crop.

Dried beef to us is "jerky." A ranking cow hand is a "top hand." A tough man or an abrasive object are either one "as rough as a cob."

Tennis shoes are frequently "tennies." For example, a customer wishing to ascertain their price will ask of the storekeeper, "What you got on tennies today?"

In the East Texas backwoods, a delicate person never says diaper. Instead he uses the word "hippen." A young mother in church, inflamed with ecclesiastical zeal, may turn to her neighbor and say, "Hold my baby while I shout." Also in East Texas you hear "holp" for help, from the Anglo-Saxon *holpen*.

Such a catalogue of indigenous expressions could be continued almost indefinitely. This sample is given here simply as an indication that a Texas language does exist, and is blending with and enriching the English language in its larger aspects.

By no means disassociated from our idiom are our local beliefs, such as that a garden of peas planted when the moon is "in flower" will bloom profusely but make no peas. We believe that if it thunders in February, it will frost in April; that to plant cotton in May instead of April will "save two choppin's and one pickin'."

A dying mule goes to the corner of the barn or lot to breathe his last. A sow picks the coldest night in the season to bear her young. Sardines are reputed to rid our dogs of worms. Many of us believe that warts can be conjured off, and that a small piece of copper wire tacked in the bottom of the feed trough will cool the passion of a pen-busting sow in heat.

We believe catfish bite in the dark of the moon, and know that squirrels prefer to go abroad on a still, bright day. Fishermen, with trot lines set and baited, consider the hoot of an owl as a sign that a fish has just caught himself on the hook.

Some of us believe that a good remedy against cramps in the legs is to turn our shoes upside down before retiring. One who is afflicted with chills and fever should wrap himself tightly in a sheet, run around the house three times and jump under the bed. Thus the chill jumps into the bed and he misses it. A crick in the neck can be cured by rubbing your neck against a tree a hog has rubbed against. A pan of kerosene under the bed helps relieve rheumatism. To prevent nightmares, we stick matches in our hair on retiring. If we cross the matches, we have no headaches. A bag of asafetida worn around the neck is supposed to ward off disease. It will certainly ward off close contact with anything possessing a nose.

Our Apostolic Church people look upon either bobbed female hair or traffic with doctors as a sin. And it is a known fact that a missing arm or a crooked leg will fetch more votes in a country election than any other issue. To ensure our luck in the twelve months to come, we eat blackeyed peas on New Year's Day.

To such beliefs there is no end. But the most persistent of these is that nowhere on earth is there such a heller, in any of the important categories from the more straightforward aspects of *l'amour* to windmill fixin', as a Texan.

12. Free-For-All

ONE of the things that has given Texans more pleasure than anything else, has provided us with more fist fights and opportunities to lose our tempers, is, as you may very well already know, politics. For years, many of our most talented citizens have devoted themselves to enlivening this pastime of the electorate, giving bounce and flavor to this greatest of our spectator sports.

Nobody has ever had more natural talent for the ungentle art of politickin' than old Sam Houston. If flashy costumes, high-voltage oratory, and eccentric behavior were required to catch the people's attention, he could supply them. And for that reason, as much as for any of the more substantial ones, Sam was twice President of the Republic and once governor of the state after Texas went into partnership with the United States. Stephen Austin, who might have felt these honors were due him, but could never intoxicate the electorate with his personality as Sam could, died in office as Houston's secretary of state.

As the parade of the years marched by, the next noteworthy political figure in Texas politics was James S., the father of Miss Ima, Hogg, a New Dealing governor of great candle-power indeed. But, until the very present, the entertainment quotient, the low comedy aspects of Texas politics, has not been lost, nor ceased to pay dividends.

The fact that we are again at war calls to mind a certain local constable race, just preceding the first world war. One of our candidates was asked how he stood on the "preparedness" question.

The candidate, a man of little learning but great caution, paused and thought, then replied, "Well, Mr. Earnest, I'll tell you. There's some things I'm *fer* repairin, and others I'm *agin'* repairin."

Had our ex-Governor (now Senator) Lee O'Daniel been even slightly less astute, had he made a slightly less careful analysis of his own talents and the emotional requirements of his constituents, he might very well, and successfully, have gone on the road with a medicine show. To the observer it might still seem that that calling would have suited him better. For the Senator is an organ with many stops and ample pipes. And when he's on the stump, not many of those stops go unpulled. To a musical background supplied by his own string band, he tells of his latter-day love of Texas (to compensate for his political misfortune in having been born outside the state, he maintains that the "Lee" in his name derives from that of Robert E.) and perhaps sings one of his own compositions such as "Beautiful, Beautiful Texas." Then, that the voter may look into the Senator's secret heart, he confides that he once had a dear old mother, etc., that he thinks old folks in general (who, of course, may vote without paying a poll tax) are just jim-dandy, and he wants them every one to have a pension. He also approves one hundred per cent of the Lord God Jehovah, widows, orphans, low taxes, the Ten Commandments, and the Golden Rule.

Though O'Daniel gets votes in present-day Texas on the basis of his Bible pounding, such was not the case in the old days. Representative of the view of many were the words of one old Texan named Bunk Turner who, when asked where he was going, poetically replied:

> Whar the grass grows and the water runs
> And the sound of the gospel never comes.

O'Daniel is opposed to "wild-eyed labor leaders," the devil, and "the professional politicians"—the somewhat indigestible inference being that he is an amateur. Since his elevation from the governorship to

the United States Senate, he reports to us by radio
that there's no place like home, and the eggs in Washington are not fresh and nice like those in Texas. But he
carries on bravely and has not requested the homefolks
to put somebody else in the job.

Yet when the foregoing has been said about O'Daniel,
all of the worst and half of the truth has been told.

There is another side of him—and God, I suppose,
Who gave him his joyous talent for campaigning, must
be on that side. For however much public hamming
O'Daniel does, there are two people who are going to
enjoy it. One is O'Daniel and the other is you. The
things he says may insult your intelligence, but the way
he says them will amuse and entertain you, leave
hovering about you the kind of glow that only the most
talented and eager entertainer leaves with you. Too,
there is a kind of pulpit sweet-sadness which, at artfully
selected intervals, creeps into O'Daniel's voice and
makes a lot of his listeners feel good. In the old days
when they went to church they built up an emotional
need for this kind of thing, so that, after hearing W. Lee,
they are pervaded by a feeling of righteousness, of having
been emotionally cleansed, and about thirty per cent
baptized.

Texas never forgets the hour of the O'Daniel broad-
casts, because it is fun to listen, because O'Daniel has
all the enthusiasm and spontaneity of Kay Kyser, and,
in addition, a kind of boldness which never lost anybody
any votes in Texas.

In any case, so far as the Texas political scene is

concerned, O'Daniel is a Johnny-come-lately. The man who has fought in this arena for twenty-five years and never been stripped entirely of power, the man who has agitated Texas most, and governed it most, is ex-Governor James E. (The Farmer's Friend) Ferguson.

Excepting only salty old Sam Houston, Jim Ferguson is, beyond all question, the greatest political figure Texas ever produced. Jim is the best writer of platforms, the best stump speaker, and best political-machine designer, operator, and mechanic that ever hit Texas.

At fifteen Jim left his Bell County home and went to the West coast. His experiences there were not unlike those of Jack London. Jim, too, was a waiter, miner, dish washer, lumberjack, bridge worker, etc. A few years later he was back in Texas working on a pile-driving crew on the Katy railroad, traveling up and down the line, shaking hands everywhere, making acquaintances who'd never forget him, whose names he'd never forget. Then he began to read law, passed the bar, began to practice in Bell County and to accumulate money and business and banking interests.

One day in answer to a newspaper article which had said that no anti-Prohibitionist was morally qualified to act as governor of the state, Jim wrote a letter to the papers saying this was irrelevant poppycock, that what the state needed as executive material was a lawyer with wide business experience. As an example he mentioned a friend of his with these qualifications. But the letters and telegrams that came pouring in urged Jim to be not a kingmaker, but king in person.

At this time Jim (according to his own account) was worth about $400,000, had 2,500 acres of black land, controlling interest in ten Central Texas banks—in a word, enough.

He decided to run for governor, and this, on the first of his "pore folks" platforms, he proceeded to do. Not yet had his fight with the University of Texas begun; not yet had he become the champion of "the little red schoolhouse" against the suave cruelties of the State University. One of his principal vote-getting planks was his declaration against the practice of landlords in charging tenants bonus payments in excess of the landlord's customary share of the crop. For where the land was extra good, such bonus payments had been the practice.

Jim knew exactly what this issue meant to the large, sharecropping element of our electorate. He could movingly translate it to them in terms of new bonnets, shoes for the children, bolts of bright gingham, occasional dishes of fresh meat in the summertime.

And he was elected.

During his campaigns Jim became the darling of the stump-speech *aficionados*. Only once, while running for his second term, did an opponent ever so much as pink his tough, resilient exterior.

On that occasion Jim's opponent declared: "They tell me that down at the Governor's Mansion, Mrs. Ferguson has got a *social secretary*." In many of our localities that would be a considerably more serious charge against a governor's wife than, say, forging checks. "But," continued the speaker, "if you put me in the governor's office, there won't be any such high-toned goin's on down there. My wife won't have any social secretary to keep you good ladies of the state from visitin' her. She ain't that kind. Whenever you are nice enough to come to see her, you won't even have to knock on the door. Just come on around the house and you'll find *my* wife in the back yard makin' soap."

Here was an arrow that might have been drawn from Jim's own quiver. Nevertheless Jim was re-elected.

Meanwhile rumors concerning the way Jim was running the state for his own benefit began spreading across the Texas prairies. As the months passed, those rumors grew. The inevitable result (inevitable since Joe Bailey, the only Texas Senator with enough influence to save Jim, was now grimly seated on the other side of the fence) was that the Texas Senate sat as a high court of impeachment, and Jim stood before them plastered with twenty-one charges.

The charges, besides one alleging that Jim took $5,600 out of a certain school fund, were most of them only malfeasance; such charges as having his appointees deposit state monies in a Temple bank in which Jim owned a quarter of the stock. This was against the law: the money should have been kept in the state treasury. But, in any case, all the state lost was the interest on this money, which, I might add, wasn't doing at all badly. On this charge, the Senate had the goods on Jim. Also on another one in which he had violated the law that says no bank can lend more than a third of the amount of its capitalization to one client. Jim had had the Temple bank lend him sums considerably in excess of its entire capitalization. Not only did the inquisitors catch him in this, the prosecution pointed out the embarrassing fact that, in a prior investigation, Jim had perjured himself on this point.

One of the most interesting charges concerned a certain $186,000 in currency that had found its way into Jim's pocket at a time when every bit of collateral he could rake and scrape was already posted on some $250,000 worth of debts.

On this point Jim refused to testify. The Senate voted to compel him to testify. He still refused. The prosecution therefore held that, after mortgaging everything else he had, Jim had mortgaged his influence as governor of the state.

The Senate found him guilty on ten of the twenty-one charges and kicked him out of office.

But that was only the beginning. Soon, since the Senate had written into the impeachment that Jim could never again hold a public office of honor and trust in the state, he ran his wife for governor. The principal issue: to vindicate Jim.

Now it would appear in retrospect that the people of Texas were the most addle-headed voters imaginable when they elected Mrs. Miriam A. ("Ma") Ferguson to the governor's chair. Well, it wasn't as simple as that. Texans are only human, and all humanity loves, and can't help loving, a fighter that won't be beat.

Old Jim might be untrustworthy, but he kept his tail up, and that got us. He had never admitted his guilt, never stopped fighting or lost his touch as a demagogue.

Illustrative of Jim's virtuosity on the witness stand is the occasion on which he was charged with filing exorbitant expenses on an allegedly official journey he made to New York. "Gentlemen," Jim replied, "when I, as a farm boy, went in to Temple to spend the night, I slept in the wagon yard. Then I was representing Jim Ferguson. In New York I was representing the great state of Texas. And I thought nothing those Yankees had was too good for the Governor of Texas."

In our state it doesn't take much of that kind of talk to get people whooping and hollering.

Largely on the strength of such antics, we elected Jim's wife to the governor's office not only once but twice. Here was an opportunity for a great fighter to show that, when the heat was really on, he was also a great man. By establishing a record of scrupulous honesty, Jim could pay us back for the warmth we'd felt for him when he was down and out.

During this second period of "Fergusonism" in Texas, the House of Representatives appointed a committee to investigate "certain departments of the state government." Some of the most promising witnesses could not—by any means open to the committee—be coerced into coming before it. A good many, however, did, and on the testimony given by these witnesses a fabulous report was offered by the committee to the House of Representatives:

" . . . we believe that the testimony is sufficient to establish the fact that the power and prestige of the Governor's office of this State, during the years 1925 and 1926, have been practically usurped, and dictated by a private citizen, the husband of the Governor, for political favoritism and financial gain, and the fact that he was a private citizen has placed him beyond the pale of the law. . . . It is our opinion . . . that the only recourse under our existing laws, is by impeachment for the wrongs done to our State by the Chief Executive under the domination of her husband. . . .

"Newspaper Activities

" . . . The first outstanding and bold effort to commercialize the Governor's office came through what was generally known as the 'Good Will' edition of the Ferguson Forum, a weekly newspaper, shown to have been then owned, edited and published by James E. Ferguson, his wife, Miriam A. Ferguson, his daughter, Mrs. George S. Nalle and Miss Dorrace Ferguson, also a daughter. . . . Road contractors, road equipment and material dealers, railroad and other public service corporations, insurance companies, oil companies, and many other private and corporate interests were the largest contributors of this plan of advertising. . . .

" . . . we quote from the testimony from W. Broadnax, one of the owners of the American Road Company. . . . Mr. Broadnax stated that when Mr. Furst, advertising solicitor for the Forum "Good Will" edition, visited his office in Dallas, the following conversation took place. After introducing himself to Mr. Broadnax, Mr. Furst said:

" 'The Governor and James E. Ferguson both have known you. You have been friends all your life.'

"Mr. Broadnax: 'Is that so?'

"Mr. Furst: 'Mr. Broadnax, I am getting out a 'Good Will' edition of the Forum. I understand you people gave twenty thousand dollars to the Ku Klux. [Ferguson and the Ku Klux were at war.] We are going to bury the hatchet, and get together and put this good road campaign over, and have lots of money to build good roads. I don't mean to say by this, that you are going to get contracts, but if you will advertise, you will get work, and everything will be on the square.'

" . . . the Ferguson Forum prior to Mrs. Ferguson's election as Governor . . . carried a very limited amount of advertising, but after her election, this paper secured an enormous amount of advertising, paid for at fabulous rates. In fact, there was no stipulated rate fixed for the advertising above discussed, only the ability and willingness of the person or corporation to pay. . . .

"Railroad Employment

" . . . just prior to the inauguration of Mrs. Ferguson as Governor of Texas, . . . W. T. Eldridge, who at that time owned extensive railroad and corporate interests in this State . . . [engaged] James E. Ferguson . . . as his personal representative for the year 1925, for which he paid Mr. Ferguson ten thousand dollars in cash, . . . requiring of Mr. Ferguson not more than five days of service each month.

" . . . We believe that . . . the contract involved a pure purchase and sale of executive influence. . . .

"Pardons

"Not in the history of organized government of our beloved State has there been such a disgraceful disregard for the proper and just punishment of criminals, and the safeguard of the people and property of this State, as has been shown by the Governor of Texas, in the past two years of her indiscriminate and super-liberal pardoning policy. We . . . believe . . . that this policy cannot be charged to the feminine sympathy of a woman Governor. . . . It appears that the principal thing that the Governor had to do was to sign her name on the dotted line, and . . . pardons have been granted in which James E. Ferguson actually signed the Governor's name. . . .

"Free Textbook Contracts

" . . . The undisputed evidence before this committee shows that James E. Ferguson, the husband of the Governor, had himself elected clerk of the State Textbook Commission, a position not provided for by law, . . . [and that] the State Textbook Commission . . . is paying more for spellers in enormous quantities than the same book can be bought at retail, one copy at a time, and shipped to Texas by mail. . . .

"Highway Department

" . . . Following the inauguration of Mrs. Ferguson as Governor, in January 1925, it became the privilege of the Executive to appoint three Highway Commissioners. . . . the three commissioners, by agreement among themselves, and not by any authority of law, divided the State into three districts; one district for each member*. . . . Contracts or agreements were entered into without publicity, . . . there was no competitive bidding, and no bond to guarantee faithful performance, and thus more than six million dollars of the people's money was awarded to . . . two firms, or companies, . . . practically in secret. Had these particular contracts been let to the lowest and best bidder, there is no doubt that the same work could have been bid in at a price practically one-third that paid by the State. . . .

"The testimony of numerous witnesses shows beyond a doubt that James Ferguson absolutely dominated the affairs of the Highway Commission. . . . [And] that the Governor . . . even went to the limit of employing private counsel out of the law enforcement fund of this State to go into the district court in an effort to prevent the Attorney General from forfeiting these iniquitous contracts. . . .

" . . . the majority of contractors obtaining contracts with the Highway Commission, made bond with

---

* One commissioner, a Mr. Bickett, was held by the Committee to be without blame in the awarding of these contracts.

[the American Surety] Company, the daughter of the Governor, Mrs. George S. Nalle, acting as the agent. . . .

"Highway Employes

" . . . The testimony shows that . . . men were discharged, who were experienced in road affairs, and their places filled with political friends of James E. Ferguson. . . .

"Highway Commission Ignores Board of Control

"The testimony of the members of the Board of Control . . . shows that the Highway Commission of this State has often ignored the law, providing for purchases to be made by the Board of Control, and that where the Board of Control refused to submit to the domination of the Highway Commission, [it made] a fraudulent rent contract for so many months with the understanding that the article rented, would belong to the State at the end of the rent period. . . . "

A few weeks ago I went down to Austin to see old Jim. He has a three-room office in the Nalle Building (remember the name?) in Austin. Jim is an old man now. He's deaf, his complexion unhealthily rosy, his lower lip swollen, drooping. But he still wears a black string tie and a big black hat, and holds himself well erect.

After we had talked a while of general matters (we'd been interrupted several times by out-of-town partisans coming up to shake old Jim's hand, say a few words and go away, by periodic telephone conversations about pardons which made it plain that Jim was still lobbying), Jim leaned back in his chair, pushed his hat off of his forehead, and said, "Son, one of the best pieces of political strategy I ever pulled off was last year when I put Lee O'Daniel in the United States Senate to serve Senator Sheppard's unexpired term, and Coke Stevenson in the Governor's chair."

For some reason, underestimating his boldness, I'd thought he'd refuse to discuss this subject. Therefore, I hadn't broached it myself.

"How did it happen?" I asked.

"Well I always liked Coke Stevenson," Jim said, "and it occurred to me one day that if we could get O'Daniel in the United States Senate, Coke, as lieutenant governor, would automatically become governor. Lots of people didn't know that. They thought if O'Daniel went to the senate, an election would have to be called to select a governor of Texas.

"Well, O'Daniel wasn't doing any good. He was losing every day. Polls showed it and so did somep'n else I'm coming to. I called up Coke and said, 'How come you ain't out there helpin' O'Daniel get elected to the senate so you can be governor?'

" 'I don't know,' Coke said. 'I hadn't thought much about it.'

" 'Well you better get busy,' I said. 'Better take to the stump and let all your friends know that a vote for O'Daniel is a vote for Stevenson. (Stevenson hadn't any important enemies.) Call up O'Daniel and tell him you're ready to go to work for him.'

"Well Coke, he called him up, but O'Daniel said, 'Nothin' doin.' He wanted to make all the speeches himself. I got in touch with O'Daniel's campaign manager and said, 'What's wrong with you folks? How come you're foolin around and gonna lose this election?'

" 'Well mainly,' he said, 'we ain't got any money. Got a radio speakin' engagement tomorrow night in Temple and we can't pay for radio time.'

" 'How much is it?' I said.

" 'Sixty-seven dollars.'

"Well that just goes to show you how things was goin. O'Daniel looked so bad as a candidate, had so little chance of winnin', that nobody'd put up any money on him. I dug sixty-seven dollars out of my pocket and give it to him and said, 'Here, go pay for it with this.' But he only took twenty and said he'd try to get the rest somewhere else in a hurry.

"Now busted campaigns weren't anything new to me. I'd been over the road before. I come back to my office and sat down to write a article. I just made two points. Figured if I made any more, it might confuse people. First I said a vote for O'Daniel was a vote for Stevenson, and, second, if the old folks wanted to keep O'Daniel in Austin to rustle pensions for them, they'd be makin a mistake. I said Coke Stevenson was a pension man too and that he'd look out for 'em in Texas, but that if they sent O'Daniel to the United States Senate, why there he'd have the privileges of the . . . er . . . "

(I thought he was going to say of the United States Treasury). Finally he added, "delivering himself on the Senate floor in Washington.

"Then," old Jim went on, "I rustled around among my hog herd and raised about seven hundred dollars and had that statement printed in the five leading newspapers of the state. Folks that read the newspapers vote. The papers had a circulation of seven hundred and fifty thousand. To be conservative, I figured two readers for every paper. That made a million and a half readers. I figured the idea was good and that it was well disseminated. I set back to wait for results."

It was hard to think of Jim sitting back, once he'd entered the contest, particularly when his opposing manipulator, the man behind the New Deal's Lyndon Johnson, was as worthy and cunning a foe as Franklin Roosevelt.

What Jim actually did was quite simple—if you know how.

First he analyzed his situation. Here was O'Daniel dying to get into the Senate. Yet Roosevelt's Johnson was going to beat him if something wasn't done. Martin Dies and Gerald Mann could not win.

But in order for the pension-hungry electorate to release O'Daniel from his job as governor, where as yet he'd not delivered on his pension promises, those promises had to be made good. Obstructing the passage of these issues were the Texas legislators, to most of whom O'Daniel's alimentary canal was a hated object.

Well maybe Jim could handle the legislators. But why? For love?

Who, particularly, might want to get O'Daniel kicked upstairs?

Jim didn't have to ponder over that one. He knew the answer well. A war was in the offing. And while one dry senator in Washington might do little harm to the beer and whisky business in Texas, one dry wartime governor such as O'Daniel could knock it cold.

That idea suggested a source of eager revenue.

Then by doing first things first and second things second, Jim helped whip O'Daniel's pension measures through the legislature. Now the people were ready to let O'Daniel go forth to Washington and perform yet greater miracles.

Coke Stevenson, under definite obligation to Jim, was ready to step into the governor's chair.

Everything was set and rigged, and then the people of Texas marched to the polls and behaved eccentrically.

In the first returns, Johnson looked like a cinch. But O'Daniel refused to cede the election. Then as the backwoods votes trickled in, O'Daniel drew almost abreast of Johnson.

"The people who counted the election returns of the last 20,000 votes," said a story in the Waco *Herald-Tribune*, "were very puzzled as returns came in from the far places whipping Governor O'Daniel into victory by a few hundred votes. But Ferguson was not puzzled by this, nor were the brewers. These things have happened before in the life of Governor Ferguson.

. . . [He] is a past master in finishing up an election to his satisfaction if an election is close enough."*

But in order to make the election legal, it had only to be certified by Senator-Elect O'Daniel. And this, at the end of whatever deliberations, Senator-Elect O'Daniel did.

So O'Daniel went to Washington, Stevenson to the Governor's Mansion, and wily old Jim Ferguson crossed home plate standing up.

So much for the man behind the throne. What of the man on it?

I went to see him recently, in company with Harry Crozier, Governor Stevenson's Minister-without-portfolio, press agent and, more recently, head of the State Unemployment Commission.

As we walked into the capitol, I was, as usual, proud of it. This building cost Texas three million acres of land. But Texans did get a building for their money.

It's made of pink granite, which sounds gaudy and ugly and isn't. Inside it, like the state it represents, there's plenty of room. On the marble floors beneath its stately dome are many impressive, inlaid doodads. On its walls are many portraits of Texas bigwigs of yesterday. But the most delightful is that of Sam Houston who, in a Caesarean mood, took off his clothes and, wrapping himself in an old blanket in lieu of a toga, had himself painted full length in the Roman style.

* The newspaper story from which the above was quoted was given to me not without a certain pride by Jim Ferguson himself.

The office of the governor is on the second floor and as we walked into the reception room, I asked Harry Crozier, "How long is Stevenson going to stay in office?"

"There's not a man in Texas," he said, "who can beat Coke in the next election. Maybe he couldn't have been elected governor in the first place, but he got a break and got here and he's gonna stay. At least for another term."

I thought that was likely. As Jim Ferguson had pointed out to me, Coke Stevenson hadn't the wealth of enemies of a governor who's just fought a hard campaign. Besides, he was now in a position to grant favors and patronage. A little earlier the subject had come up in conversation with Harry and he'd said, "Even before he'd got this office, Coke always said he'd make sound, well qualified appointments, but he also said there'd probably be at least one good reliable Stevenson man among the candidates and that the good Stevenson man would get the job."

If Coke Stevenson were of the Ferguson school, I knew that would be a first principle. Jim never forgot a political friend, never let a henchman go unrewarded.

"Come on in," Harry said. "Let's see Coke."

When we went in, some photographers were in the Governor's office taking his picture. He was a bad poser. Stiff. The photographers couldn't get him to hold his pipe right. The Governor insisted on pretending to be working. He said he didn't want the people over the state to think he just sat around with his feet on the desk. As a matter of fact he had been busy before the picture-taking started, trying to finish that week's copy of *Time*.

He had an extremely interesting face. It had manifest political value in that it represented something that was truly Texan. Coke Stevenson looked like a Westerner, a rancher. Just as manifestly, he was a cool, cautious man. His eyes were intelligent and clear. Aside from a mild, surface good humor, I got the feeling of an interior stoniness.

My chat with the Governor was pleasant. I felt he was less gifted politically than either the sage Jim Ferguson or the bright-eyed songster, O'Daniel. Nevertheless I rather liked him and thought I'd probably vote for him for governor at the next election. Whenever the conversation deviated from a homespun tone, Harry Crozier carefully restored it.

I wondered what ultimate objective the Crozier-Stevenson team had in mind. For Crozier is sharp and imaginative and loyal. He professes to sense many Lincolnian characteristics in Stevenson. But Harry Crozier is sometimes a man of large enthusiasms.

Stevenson might make a very good, definitely ornamental vice-president of the United States. More likely what they have in mind is the United States Senate a few years hence, when the people have become bored with the buffoonery of O'Daniel, the flour salesman, or, as a certain old Bohemian from La Grange who'd been listening to O'Daniel's radio antics once spoke of him—and quite seriously too—"that biscuit man what's in the air."

Also itching to pick off O'Daniel's job is ex-Governor (now Judge) James V. Allred. But Coke Stevenson would look more like a senator from Texas. And, despite the fact that he bears the benediction of Jim Ferguson, he may one day make the grade in those semi-finals of United States politics.

13. Black Magic

A DOZEN years ago Northeast Texas was a very sad, down-at-the-heel sight indeed. The noble forests of short leaf, long leaf, and loblolly pine that had once blanketed this portion of Texas were by this time cut-over wastelands on which white and Negro share-croppers tried to raise cotton out of the sterile, red land. The houses, leaning against trees, or simply relaxing and falling down, appeared generally to be beyond habitation. This region was distinguished by its sawmill ghost towns, razorback hogs, hungry children and hungry hounds. Its spiritual affiliation was not with Texas, but with the Old South and the backwardness thereof.

It did have a couple of "world's mosts." Tyler, which regarded itself as capital of the realm, grew more roses than any other spot on earth. Jacksonville had the world skinned on tomato production. There were also extensive and more or less profitable and sizable peach orchards in Morris County, but the spirit of the section was one of decay.

It had a good many million tons of iron ore, but nobody took the trouble to convert it into metal. Its hopes of petroleum deposits had long since been blasted by the geologists who had satisfied themselves that help was not to be had from this source. Then, in 1930, God Almighty, through the agency of a wildcatter named "Dad" Joiner, hit East Texas in the rump with a chain of lightning.

Dad brought in a well near Turnertown in Rusk County, a "gusher," as the uninitiated speak of it, and the lid was off. Wells were cheap to dig (only thirty-six hundred feet through soft rock) and it soon became apparent that East Texas had a new "world's most" of the very first magnitude to hang on its belt. The world's richest oil field had been discovered under the peanut and sweet potato patches.

But the East Texas field comes late in the story of Texas oil. Its beginning lies in the voracious hunger of men for wealth.

Let's suppose I had a job cooking hamburgers or taking the morning papers off a night train, or that I was a county official or an imaginative storekeeper (it hardly matters what). I knew a way to make myself the most powerful and glittering man in my community, to have a fine house with telephone plugs by every chair, to control the credit, virtually the destiny, of my neighbors. I could make them knuckle under and tug their locks. My home could become the social center of the town. I could put myself in a position to make or break them every one. I could indulge any whim that came to me if I had enough money. And one of the fastest ways to get enough is in oil.

Of course, I might be one of those rare oil men like A. M. Phelan, of Beaumont. I might look upon my millions in solemn thankfulness and humility of spirit. Like him, I might succor the poor, patronize the arts to the extent of my ability, give hundreds of thousands of dollars to the propagation of the Christian faith.

There are, beyond question, some honest people who've made millions in oil, who never so much as paid or accepted a bribe. Some Texas oilmen get sick at the thought of graft, as did a Mr. Mooers of Houston. He wanted his allowable (the amount of oil he was allowed to draw from his wells each day) raised and was told by a minion of the Railroad Commission that, for five grand, it could be arranged. Mooers, agreeing, brought five thousand dollars in marked currency to a hotel room, and handed it over. When the newly prosperous representative of our state regulatory machinery stepped out of the door, he was nabbed, relieved of the five thousand, and hustled off to the calaboose.

But the oil industry is by no means composed exclusively of Mooers and Phelans. If I, as an oil operator, were a normal but impressionable young man who'd found myself in a business climate where I was constantly seeing commercial piracy, mixed with a little shrewdness and some luck, being turned into huge, fast fortunes all around me, I might very well be tempted into playing the same game. If I were originally a honky-tonk bouncer or an ordinary clever chiseller, the probability is I'd be hungry for power, and a display of power, and, if I could keep out of jail, I'd get it. For I very likely would have told a thousand lies, worked skin games, been bribed and have paid bribes, to have got quick millions in the first place. Because into its fold the oil business in Texas has invited and accepted some of the most talented, simon-pure thieves that ever perjured themselves in any of the spectacular expansion periods of any of the new American industries.

The gold rushes may have fostered a little more physical violence. The great periods of expansion in railroads and public utilities may have fostered a little more bribery of public officials, but I don't for a second believe it. Surely none of these enterprises drew upon sharper talents or easier consciences than the oil business in Texas.

That the total benefit accruing to the nation from these shenanigans is tremendous, nobody cares to deny. Moreover, if a new national resource or service potentiality as quickly lucrative as oil were discovered tomorrow, the amount of chicanery incident to its exploitation would no doubt be somewhere near as great. For oil in itself is very innocent stuff, a collection of hydrocarbon molecules of differing sizes and characters, none of which means anybody any especial harm.

Some people say that in the geological yesterday huge quantities of vegetation were caught in vast pockets, and that time and heat and pressure converted it into petroleum. Other people say it was animal matter thus trapped. Some say it was both. Still others who've tried to find out admit they don't know.

In any case, in 1901, when the "Lucas Gusher" came in at Spindletop near Beaumont (the first big Texas field), it blew oil all over the countryside. After a few more fields were discovered, the price of crude oil dropped to an all-time low of three cents a barrel.

The refineries, seeking to make a good lamp fuel out of the raw product, were embarrassed by the presence of certain lighter, more volatile hydrocarbons (natural gasoline), which blew up lamps right and left.

Came finally the internal-combustion engine. And gasoline had found a use. But only the natural gasoline was recovered from the crude oil. From what was left a little semi-greasy lubricating oil and axle grease were extracted. The ultimate residuum was used for fuel oil and to settle the dust on near-by roads.

Although production had run entirely away from burgeoning consumption, it was not long before consumption caught up with it, and the race was on for the discovery of new fields. Burkburnett, Ranger, Mexia, all these fields attracted to themselves thousands of "boomers"—people who followed the oil booms: laborers, moonshiners, whores, gamblers, jackleg lawyers, drillers, men on the indiscriminate make.

Meanwhile, every phase of the oil business was mushrooming. Refineries were being built. Pipe lines were being laid by human elephants. These were the toughest of the oil field people: the weight lifters, the weather defiers, big men, strong, tough beyond description, sowing the earth with steel arteries a foot, two feet, in diameter.

Amateur geologists were cropping up everywhere. In my town a man brought in a peculiar mineral. Over it two of our amateur geologists labored for weeks, pulverizing, analyzing. At last, baffled, they gave up, and asked the man exactly where he'd found it. "Scarbrough and Hicks grocery store," he said. It was a cake of Bon Ami.

My father, a merchant, excited by the thought of great profits, took a train trip to Beaumont to inspect the Spindletop field. At the last stop short of the oil city, a passenger stuck his head out and inquired the name of the town.

"Liberty," a native answered.

"Give me death," the passenger said, and closed the window.

At the cigar counter in the Crosby House at Beaumont, my father saw a man in the act of paying for a cigar out of a huge roll of bills. The man discovered a five-dollar bill in the roll, accused it of being unwanted chicken feed, tore it up, and threw it in the spittoon.

And since Spindletop was near tidewater, the great refineries, refineries that now process a half million barrels of crude oil a day, were located at Beaumont and Port Arthur. Others of the first magnitude were placed at Baytown and Houston.

The stage was set for the East Texas discovery, and the discovery was made. The crib door was open and the swill barrel full. Here were inestimable riches that would go to the fastest smartest, manipulator.

If any man stood in the way of my getting what I considered my part, I "took care of him" in any of hundreds of ways.

How did I go about it? Well, the oil lies under the land, and I knew I had to lease the land to get the oil. But I couldn't afford to lease all the land. I had to do selective leasing, and yet to me all land looked alike.

It was common knowledge that certain big companies had seismograph crews working. These crews were working out sub-surface geological structures by shooting dynamite vibrations into the earth and seeing how promptly they bounced back. If they bounced back much more quickly in one spot than others near by, the presence of a salt dome was indicated. (A salt dome is, roughly, a cone-shaped pocket in which oil is frequently trapped.)

First, to save trouble, I tried to bribe the man who tabulated the findings of the seismograph crew to give me the information I wanted. I did it subtly so that he could take it or leave it and not have an obvious right to be offended. If he didn't choose to be bribed, I then had his maps stolen. That failing, I bribed the map maker who struck off duplicates for the oil company.

If that didn't work, I bribed the archivist who kept the maps in the oil company office. He didn't have to steal them for me. I would be satisfied with a photostatic copy.

With this information, I took a lease, promoted a well, and, if I struck oil, I was rich. I now could shoot dice at five thousand dollars a throw in the better Houston gambling houses, and " bug" the eyes of all present. I was a success and a leader in the community.

Suppose I were a lease broker. The best person, then, to bribe was the head land man of one of the big companies. When his company was about to take a 12,000- or 15,000-acre block, he tipped me off. I leased land in the middle of the proposed block for fifty cents an acre. I didn't want to seem greedy, so I only leased a couple of thousand acres. (If I took too much, they might abandon this block and leave me holding a bag full of leases.) I then held out on my confederate's company until, in order to complete its block, it bid fifteen dollars an acre for my leases. If I split even with the company land man, my net profit was $14,500. His half I delivered to him in cash, out of my suitcase, at a Houston hotel.

There are many variants of this procedure, but the same principle of collusion generally obtains and is responsible not only for some sizable Texas fortunes, but some discharged, black-listed, head land men.

When the East Texas field came in, it was so mammoth that with all wells running wide open the market was soon flooded and the price of oil dropped very near to zero. Steps had to be taken to restrain this flood, and the state Railroad Commission was empowered to arrest and prorate the flow. The chief fruit of this action was the term "hot oil," a comprehensive phrase referring not only to oil flowed in excess of the official allowable but stolen oil as well.

In avoiding the wrath of the Railroad Commission, an office which, by the way, is fraught with the most paralyzing temptations, every conceivable means was used, and many of them with success.

If I had a well under the scrutiny of one of the minions of the Railroad Commission, and I didn't care to broach certain delicate subjects to him, I just had a little plumbing done the first time he went into town. That is to say, I connected a pipe onto the well at a level below that at which inspection occurred, and then I let her flow.

For that matter, if my neighbor had a lease super-intendent who was drawing two hundred dollars a month, I might pay him five hundred dollars not to look while I also made an underground connection between my neighbor's well and my own storage tanks.

If the owner caught me at it, I probably knew something on him that would keep him quiet. In any case, if a week or two had passed before he caught me flowing his well, I'd made a very decent little fortune.

On all of this hot oil, of course, the landowner did not receive a penny of his one-eighth royalty to which, under his lease contract, he was entitled.

In many instances he had already received a first-rate skinning when his land was leased. For example, after an agreement had been reached on the terms of a lease, I may have switched the papers on him while he put on his glasses. But the principal racket, and one it will do well to remember if you own an acre of land, is this.

A wildcat (a shot-in-the-dark or blue-sky exploratory well) is being drilled within a mile or so of your land. I come to you and want to take a lease on it. I have timed my trip within a week or so of the completion of the exploratory well. You'd already been offered a dollar an acre, think it worth five, so you ask me ten.

I try, for window dressing, to beat you down on the price. But finally, though you are scared stiff that I am going to back out of the trade entirely, I let you have your way. I write something on a piece of paper binding both of us to the trade, contingent only, of course, on the validity of your title. To that you, as a fair-minded person, agree. And I've got you stretched over a barrel.

A flaw can be found in any Texas land title. The acceptance or rejection of any particular one is almost a matter of taste. If the wildcat makes a producing well, your lease is worth fifty dollars an acre up, and I take it for the agreed-upon ten. If the well fails, I don't like your title, and would like to see the color of the man's eyes that can make me pay for it.

The only way you would have had a chance was to refuse to sign anything, let me examine the title at my own risk, and take the lease or leave it.

It is an unofficial axiom of the oil people that more money is put into the ground in search of oil than is ever taken out. The loss money, it is pointed out, is usually sucker money. The smart professionals get theirs back many fold.

The stock company racket was in itself a vast and lively institution whose nemesis and Achilles heel was, oddly enough, the discovery of oil on company leases. A stock company might flourish for years, its officers drawing handsome salaries as they managed the affairs of a company drilling one dry hole after another. Yet almost invariably if the company inadvertently struck oil, the fat was in the fire. For it then became evident that, though the stockholders' dream had come true, no noticeable revenue was to be had because the stock had been fantastically oversold. At this point the postal authorities would enter the scene—the company promoters, Leavenworth.

The cornucopia of any stock company was its sucker list. A good one could be expected to yield dollars indefinitely. "They just don't learn," one expert informed me. "It's part of their natures. For example, I know of a doctor who heads every list. He's a brilliant surgeon and an intelligent man. But every time you go to him with an oil scheme, you get the money. He's been burnt a dozen times. But he never learns."

To illustrate the importance of a sucker list, this same expert told me a delightful story.

A certain Texan whom we shall call Blevins was frequently employed in a minor capacity by a stock company whose prosperity was not only obvious, but just as obviously increasing by leaps and bounds. Soon Blevins began to recognize the magic of the sucker list.

and to appropriate names from the lists of his employers. Also, borrowing the best phrases and promises from the letters he'd seen them sending out, he mailed a printed oil proposition to a thousand suckers. Among his inducements for the victim to send money was a particularly juicy lease which could not fail to produce oil.

The money poured in. He mailed another thousand letters. The flow doubled.

It was now necessary, in case somebody (his stockholders or the postal authorities) should want to see this lease, to get one and start a well. But since there was no use wasting money on an expensive lease, he went to an area where leases could be had almost for nothing, and took a big cheap one. The principal consideration in the landowner's favor was that Blevins agreed to start a well in ninety days, and drill to a specified depth. That was all right from Blevins's viewpoint because he had to bung down a well somewhere anyway. For further window trimming, he hired a tramp geologist to stake out a location for the first well. The geologist's report was oddly enthusiastic. He said the indications of finding oil were excellent. This gave Blevins pause. But he was in too deep to back out now.

He set about to hire a drilling rig. At the time, these mechanisms were scarce and many weeks were consumed in obtaining one. In fact, the ninety days had almost elapsed when movement of the machinery began. At this point torrential rains fell. Roads became quagmires. Creeks spread over everything. It became apparent that the rig could not reach the geologist's location in the center of the lease in time to begin operations by the ninetieth day, since several overflowed creeks intervened. Therefore, the well was begun on the nearest corner of the lease, a mile or so from the location established by the geologist.

The well was drilled—and blew in. Other fabulously rich wells came in on the same lease, almost everywhere on it, that is, except on the location originally staked out by the geologist. But this was one of those exceptional cases where a promotor was not ruined by discovering oil. Blevins had found such unlikely floods of it, and so early in the game, that all of his stockholders got big enough dividends to satisfy them and to circumvent any desire for an investigation by the postal authorities, as would have been the case if the discovered pool of oil had been nominal. Blevins now is a vastly rich and un-incarcerated man.

But, on the other side of the ledger, there are cases in which good faith and honesty emerged triumphant. In one section a wildcatter brought in a well on a block of land he had not leased completely. Eighty of these unleased acres belonged to a very old Negro woman named Lou. In a near-by town, however, was a banker who had known Lou for years and was determined she should receive a proper, at least an adequate, price for her mineral rights. At once he left his desk and went out to protect her interests. Acting as her adviser, he refused every blandishment of the lease hounds, every offer of joint ownership if he'd just tell the old woman to sell cheaply. Faithfully the banker stayed with her and saw that she held out until she'd been offered five hundred dollars an acre. On that basis, the deal was closed.

"Now, Aunt Lou," the banker said, "you've got forty thousand dollars. That's more than you ever dreamed of, more than you can understand. Anything you want from now on, you'll be able to buy. In this deal I've been a good friend to you, and now I'd like to buy a little of your royalty."

The old woman looked at him in astonishment.

"Lawsy mercy, Mr. Joe," she said, taken completely aback. "I ain't done nothin' like that in twenty years."

It might be interesting to look about and see what oil has made of Texans, how it has changed and shaped them.

One amateur geologist I know used to slither through the woods at night, spying on drilling crews, always convinced that they were finding oil and plugging the hole until they'd leased more land.

Another friend, in the days before trucks, drove an eight-mule team hauling oil field supplies through the country roads which were sometimes bottomless loblollies. He got paid a dollar a line, that is, eight dollars a day, and you could hear him for miles swearing happily at those mules. He was the best skinner in his part of Texas and he knew it. Those, for him, were the good, the kingly days that never returned.

Came the truckers and their assistants, the swampers, driving night and day over the vast state. For their relaxation and refreshment came the aforementioned honky-tonks, the roadside hamburger stands that furnished beer and entertainment, the former to be had downstairs. Here, unlike the whorehouses where some order was maintained and everything was on a sound financial basis, the truckers competed for the favors of the hashers with presents, with fists, and with lengths of iron pipe.

Texas' seven-thousand-pound load limit for trucks (only recently abolished) was of great assistance to the honky-tonk proprietor. For it gave him a chance to render signal services to his principal customers, the truckers.

For example, at Nick's place there was an electric sign on the roof which burned as a signal to trucks coming from any direction. If the sign were lighted, it meant the coast was clear. If it were dark, it meant highway police were in town, stopping and weighing trucks at the crossroads.

When a driver of an overloaded truck—and practically all of them were—got to Nick's, he was given the latest telephoned and truck-brought reports on that night's police activities, given a route sheet and a free cup of coffee and some doughnuts. All this was to attract his gasoline and oil and tire business. But Nick's desire to accommodate did not stop there. If the truck's big reserve tank would only take thirty-five gallons, Nick gave the driver a receipt showing he'd paid for fifty gallons so that at the end of the run, when the trucking company reimbursed him for expenses, the driver could make a little profit. It worked the same with oil and tires. Finally, if you were a really good customer, Nick would use his influence in your behalf with the hashers, with Emma or Myrtle or Holstein Nelle, as the case might be.

Besides the truckers and honky-tonks, hot oil brought a rash of little refineries, made of junk, for skimming the natural gasoline off of this contraband petroleum. Until the operators got caught and closed down, or until the expenses of diplomatic overhead ate up all the profits, it was a money-making proposition.

There was also for a long time a lively trade in stolen oil-field equipment, which is extremely expensive stuff. Generally orders were taken first. The materials were then stolen and delivered by truck at night.

But the roughnecks, the workers on the drilling rigs, were the skilled, happy-go-lucky, whisky-drinking, fist-fighting crew that gave the oil business its liveliest, most wholesome aspect. Most of them were tough, adventurous, and likeable young men who were acquainted with the interiors of many jails, and who had many notches carved on their tabulative valentines. Usually, after five or six years, they drifted into some less helter-skelter phase of the business or became operators of intricate construction machinery and later perhaps superintendents. However, many were killed by tools dropped from high in the derricks, others by slipping into the machinery on the slick derrick floor.

Yet the great period of "shush-buckling," as one famous Hollywood producer articulates the word, is now more or less over.

All is reasonably quiet on the East Texas, the Spindle-top, the Rodessa fronts. Most of the small refineries, completely unable to compete in either pecuniary or scientific resources with the major companies, have folded. The nature of the federal tax system discourages flashy flotation. Even the sure-thing boys have slowed down. The huge refineries' systems have the situation in their capable, metallic hands, and a strict economy of natural resources is being practiced.

It is true that billions of cubic feet of natural gas are still being burnt in Texas oil fields, gas that serves no good purpose except its own dissipation in the interests of safety. Yet to try either to store or move it would probably be uneconomic.

At the refineries nothing, any longer, is wasted. After the natural gasoline is distilled from the crude, a considerable residuum remains. This contains the heavier hydrocarbons from which kerosene, lubricating and fuel oils are made. But since the greatest need is for gasolines, this residuum is then "cracked." In this process the refineries make little hydrocarbon molecules out of big ones either by a combination of pressure and heat or, as in the famed Houdry process, by the use of a catalytic agent. These cracked gasolines are then regarded as blending stocks, and are mixed with natural gasoline and "casinghead" to make the kind of gasoline that automobile or aviation motors require. "Casing-head gasoline" is composed of gases captured at the oil well and reduced from a vapor to a liquid by the application of pressures and below-normal temperatures, just as steam is reduced to water.

The present-day refineries are vast, splendiferous plants strewn with strangely shaped metal globes and tubes; with skilled personnel from top to bottom. For example, a worker at the Magnolia plant in Beaumont who has only been there seven or eight years is considered a rookie. Most of the men have grown up with the technological advancements that have revolutionized refinery practice time and time again. With so little labor turnover, it has been reasonably easy for the refineries to forestall unionization—that, plus excellent treatment of the workers, excellent working conditions, and good salaries.

From live green crude oil these refineries make hundreds of products that will do any job better than the raw petroleum itself could do. Many of these items are astonishing. Vital sulfapyridine—nemesis of streptococci—doesn't grow on trees any more than money does. It's being made out of petroleum.

At Baytown, toluene is cracked from waste gases, and toluene is what the second T in TNT stands for. Medicinal mineral oils are of course an old product. Oil for soaps is not. Every imaginable kind of wax is made from petroleum, compounds for leather-dressing and for waterproofing canvas, paraffin for any of a thousand uses. Cosmetic bases are also made.

Then there are the bases of various insecticides. Oil in emulsion is sprayed on fruit to keep bugs away. The mixture is non-poisonous; the film does the trick. There are petroleum derivatives for spraying packinghouse meats to seal their exteriors against the loss of moisture or natural juices. Road and roofing materials are made from the heaviest residual hydrocarbons; so, too, is coke. Carbon black, made from waste gases, is used, along with other petroleum products, in the manufacture of artificial rubber.

The refining processes are continual, as is the flow of oil through the plants. Ships are waiting at the tidewater refineries to transport the fuels and lubricants all over the world. Ships or tank cars. And don't be surprised to see a tank car belonging to one oil company being filled with the product of a competitor. For while most refiners advertise that there is no gasoline in the universe possessing the peculiarly magical powers of theirs, that, of course, is mainly a figure of speech. It's all good, and this business of pumping one refinery's gasoline out of another refinery's service station is a mild and amiable, a completely harmless, fraud that should distress no one unduly.

And finally, if you're bothered about the oil supply's eventual and certain exhaustion, it's hardly worth the trouble. There'll always be alcohol (even if it is troublesomely apt to absorb water out of the air), huge American fields of oil-producing shale, and, finally, in Texas alone, thirty billion tons of recoverable lignite from which gasoline can be made. And by the time that this is gone, the atom will probably be harnessed and responding gingerly to such terms as gee and haw.

But oil, more than anything else, has made Texas rich, as of this our time. Both the honest men and crooks who exploited it were energetic, ingenious, daring. Already they've earned themselves and Texas many billions of dollars. At the present rate oil floods Texas with three-quarters of a billion dollars a year. It gives every landowner the right to dream, to think, "maybe they'll bore and find it out in the pasture where that funny looking water seeps out of the hill." It makes them wonder what they'd do if they had a million dollars. It puts full dress coat tails over the rumps of the oil barons when the opera comes to Dallas. It pays for most of the Scotch whisky drunk in a state that really prefers bourbon. It makes the University of Texas a thing of splendor and heft and beauty. Finally, it burns and it greases, makes Texas rich and America strong.

14. The Incomparable Smithwick

ONE of the most amusing people who ever came to
Texas was Noah Smithwick. He'd tackle anything that
offered either excitement, fun or profit, and enjoyed
life hugely. He was a rare man in many ways. But he
was principally remarkable in that at the age of ninety
he was willing to tell the truth in his autobiography,
about the exploits and escapades of his own youth.

He managed to poke his nose in just about everything
that was of interest, and since he was such a healthy,
lively, somehow decent and merry lad, a glance at his
story should give both an intimate and an entertaining
picture of personal relations at the time.

Noah hit Texas in 1827 at the age of nineteen, looking for adventure. The first people he met were a tribe of

coastal Indians, who, smeared with alligator grease to keep away the mosquitoes and several layers of dirt for no especial reason, rather gave Noah the willies. There was a loaded cannon at hand which Noah was anxious to set off among the Indians—not out of cruelty, I am certain, but mainly in order to make a large noise and to be able to say he'd killed a lot of Indians.

Proceeding farther inland, that night be cadged his first Texas meal, which was composed of dried venison and honey. Bread was a delicacy not in evidence.

As Noah went on toward Dewitt's colony, he passed many fine herds of deer. He was eager to kill himself a deer, but, though a crack shot at stationary targets, he couldn't hit a moving deer no matter how he tried.

The occasional cabins he passed were drab objects with neither floors nor windows. Each had a stick-and-mud chimney, which frequently caught fire, so that the householder had to run outside and pry it over on the ground with a pole. Land was cleared by burning off the canebrakes, prepared for planting with a sharp stick. The place, according to Noah, was "a heaven for men and dogs, but a hell for women and oxen." Gourds served as both mugs and bowls; knives were mostly hunting or butcher knives; forks were whittled out of cane. Indeed, property of any kind besides land was so meager that a man with a pig was called "Hog" Mitchell, another, with a cow, "Cow" Cooper.

Soon Noah met Colonel Austin, and since Noah had a little experience as a blacksmith, the colonel got him a job as armorer to the Mexican garrison at San Antonio.

The tools there were ancient, difficult things and since the only sweetheart he had (local society snubbed him) was a rich but ugly Mexican girl not satisfying to Noah's fastidious taste, he quit his job and pulled out of town.

His next venture was an extremely enjoyable smuggling tour into Mexico proper with five hundred pounds of tobacco. Though the Mexican customs officials stole a part of his wares (their dishonesty appalled Noah), he got the remainder across the river, bribed the *Alcalde* ('a sort of mayor'), and made arrangements for the disposal of his tobacco. But this took time, and inasmuch as his companion, a man named Webber, was a pretty good actor, they declared him to be a doctor and Noah his interpreter.

A doctor, in this time and place, was a rare and exotic creature; business, therefore, was fine. Dr. Webber's medical supplies were limited chiefly to violent physics and emetics, and when one failed to work, the other was prescribed. Both failing separately, they were then tried copiously and in conjunction. Out of these antics Noah derived much fun. For, with the arrogance of most other Texans of that time, he looked upon the Mexican patients as "scarce more than animal."

Back in Texas, no richer but a little wiser, Noah set up in the smithing business at San Felipe. As soon as Jim Bowie began to have so much luck disemboweling people with a certain kind of dirk, Noah learned to copy it, even making one for Jim, and did a thriving business, getting from five to twenty dollars per knife according to the finish.

But that was workaday stuff. Noah had the most fun after the sun went down. If there was a wedding in the offing, Noah was the first one invited. For immediately after the wedding feast there would be a dance, and Noah's office was to "torture the catgut."

The floors were made of the flat sides of split logs, but that slowed no one down. The young folks shuffled and double-shuffled, wired and cut the pigeon wing. And since it was more fun to kick up a terrific racket with your feet, the few fellows with shoes would dance awhile, then lend their more formidable footgear to those who only had moccasins.

The favorite tune was "Oh Get Up Gals in the Morning."

These functions would last until daylight and the boys would accompany the girls home, ostensibly at least to shoo off the Indians.

If the groom had any relatives round about, they would hold what was called an "infair," which simply meant doing the whole thing over.

Before long, however, one of Noah's friends killed an *Alcalde* who, in Noah's opinion, needed killing. At the public behest, Noah himself made the irons that were clamped on his friend, but the more he thought about it, the less he liked it. In the end, he gave his friend a file to cut himself loose with, some money, and a gun. But the town found out about it and banished Noah, which rather hurt his feelings.

As he left, he was in entire agreement with an erstwhile San Felipean of literary bent who'd said:

> The United States, as we understand,
> Took sick and did vomit the dregs of the land.
> Her murderers, bankrupts and rogues you may see,
> All congregated in San Felipe.

Somewhat petulantly, wishing the whole town the worst possible luck, Noah went up to the Redlands in Northeast Texas, where some fine opportunities in counterfeiting presented themselves, but Noah declined them all.

One day Noah dropped in on a court proceeding in which one man was being tried for shooting another's dog. There being no statutes at hand, counsel for defense asked the abysmally ignorant *Alcalde* if he would try the case on a basis of Mosaic law. The *Alcalde*, knowing no reason for refusing, agreed. Then turning to Deuteronomy XXIII:18, counsel for defense read: "Thou shalt not bring the hire of a whore or the price of a dog into the house of the Lord thy God; for even both of these are an abomination unto the Lord thy God."

That was enough for the *Alcalde*. Said he: "Case dismissed. Plaintiff is to pay costs."

When the war with Mexico came along, Noah was Johnny-on-the-spot. "I came of a warlike race," he says, "and all my life, like Norval, 'had heard of battles.' My father fought in the revolutionary war; one of his brothers fell in the battle of Cowpens, and there was a family tradition that my great-grandfather

Bennet, when one hundred years old, knocked a man down for hallooing, 'Hurrah for King George!' "

Noah shot himself a Mexican or two in the neighborhood of San Antonio, but he missed the big moment at San Jacinto, because his party, having encountered a herd of cows in the night and mistaking them for Mexican soldiery, had been madly retreating all over the country.

About this time Noah did a couple of hitches with the Rangers. For a year's work he was given a certificate entitling him to 1,280 acres of land. One of these he swapped for a horse which the Indians stole in a week.

Once he was sent as an ambassador to the Comanches. This work he found pleasant in most respects outside his obligation to dine upon Comanche fare.

The Comanche recipe for grilled tripe was: remove from the animal, wipe a time or two across the grass, and broil. Greatest delicacy of all, however, was the curd that was taken from the stomachs of suckling fawn or baby buffalo, at which Noah, diplomacy notwithstanding, drew the line.

But Noah's relations with the Indians were not limited to the Comanches. One night while he was present for a victory supper with a tribe of Tonkawas, the main dish was composed of equal parts of new potatoes, spring corn, and the meat of an ex-Comanche.

Yet Noah looked upon the Comanches neither as tidbits nor as paragons in the rearing of children—for when milder means failed to silence a bawling infant, particularly a captured white one, one of the braves was apt to catch it by the heels and bash its head against a tree.

Once when Noah brought a party of braves down to the town of Houston to make a treaty (one which, incidentally, neither side ever kept), the braves saw and were both fascinated and terrified by a steamboat.

"Tell 'em we've got hundreds of them," President Houston told Noah, "and that they'll run on land as well as water."

When on raiding trips against the Indians, Noah sometimes had to kill wild cattle, make boats of their hides and in them send the wounded down the rivers— any which flowed back through the settled areas.

Meanwhile Cupid had thrown an inescapable hammer lock on Noah. Deciding finally to jump the broomstick, he gave up his Ranger commission, which had never been lucrative. With his bride he moved to a place called Webber's Prairie, which took its name from "Doctor" Webber who'd settled it first.

The doctor, since Noah had last seen him, had had relations of some intimacy with a slave girl named Puss. And when Puss had a baby, the fake Dr. Webber showed the neighborhood what he was made out of. He bought Puss and married her.

At this, Webber's neighbors, not recognizing an inexpressibly courageous action when they saw one, decided to drum him out of the country. But Noah pointed out that if they did, drumming was going to come pretty hard because he intended to stand up for Webber, and that the only reason that there weren't already a good many notches on his gun was because he didn't enjoy whittling.

When a mail route was opened through Webber's Prairie, Noah was made postmaster. But his political career was to have no such meager pinnacle. Not long afterward he became the local justice of the peace and, as he says, "donned the judicial ermine."

The groom of the first couple Noah married had got caught in the rain the night before and dried out his buckskin pants by sitting before the fire. At the wedding next day, the knees of the groom's pants, according to Noah, "performed the part of ushers, as it were."

When Webber's Prairie got a schoolhouse, it had neither floor, nor windows, nor even a door. A couple of the lower logs were left uncut at the doorway. Over this barrier the smaller children had to be lifted, but it served its purpose in keeping pigs out of the classroom.

Bills of sale on cattle were used as currency. In this way, if a widow sold her cow, she delivered only the bill of sale, which passed from hand to hand, while she went right on milking the cow—eventually getting enough money to buy back the bill of sale.

As the Indians came slightly under the spell of civilization, a few affected or attempted the white man's tendencies in dress. One of the most charming pictures in the fat album of Noah's memory is that of an Indian squaw bringing her young boy to preaching and standing him in the church door. At home the boys went stark naked, but this squaw, feeling something special was in order for so august an occasion, had adorned her son in a costume "consisting only of a tiny bow of pink ribbon in lieu of the traditional fig leaf." Somewhat unnecessarily Noah adds that it "attracted much attention."

One night sitting around a campfire, an old man named Uncle Tommy told Noah he could prove that the world did not revolve. Somewhat casually, and with private amusement, Noah asked how.

Uncle Tommy then cut three stakes, lined them up with the North Star, and told Noah that anytime he cared to get up in the night they'd still be lined up with the same star. And, for the moment, Noah had nothing more to say.

In the early 1840's, the Republic of Texas was broke as usual, and was trying to get France to take a mortgage on the state's public domain. This, Noah thought, was terrible and would make Texas a vassal to France. This malignant transaction was, however, circumvented when the hostler of M. de Saligny, the French chargé d'affaires, got mad at the pigs of a Mr. Bullock. These pigs filched corn in His Excellency's stable, frequently climbing into the feed troughs and competing with His Excellency's horses for their food.

When the exasperated hostler stuck a pitchfork into one of Mr. Bullock's pigs and threw it over the fence, local feeling reached such a point that not only did Mr. Bullock thrash the hostler, but ordered the indignant chargé d'affaires off the Bullock premises when he came to complain. Then when the Texas government failed to give M. de Saligny satisfaction, he demanded his passport, switched out of the state, and went back to France—all negotiations on the financial treaty which was so odious to Noah coming thereby to an abrupt and final end.

A little later on, getting interested in water-driven mills, and recalling that unofficially he had invented the mill-driven circular saw, Noah began building himself a series of mills, which every now and again would wash away.

The most fun he had during these milling days was going to political gatherings. Weeks in advance a committee would be formed to assess the countryside for viands. Millers gave quantities of flour, the grocers what could not elsewhere be had. One farmer would bring a wagon load of roasting ears, another a load of watermelons, others cantaloupes and such vegetables as the country afforded. Ranchers furnished beef and pork in huge quantities. Hunters brought in venison and turkeys. The women baked wild grape and plum and dewberry pies.

A brush arbor would be built, a speaker's stand and seats erected, the ground floor covered with sawdust for dancing later. And everybody came, those not having conveyances trudging in on foot.

The first event was a national salute fired from holes bored in the rocks. Then a fiddler played "Yankee Doodle" and "Hail Columbia."

"The literary exercises began with a reading of the Declaration of Independence" by a fourteen-year-old lad.

Then the orator of the day took the stand and orated for hours.

"At last it was finished, and the famished multitude made a rush for the dinner which had long been waiting, the odor therefrom aggravating the impatience of the throng, to a large number of which the dinner was the principal feature of the occasion, presumably having risen early and breakfasted on anticipation of the feast."

Well before night the seats were moved out and the dancing began. It, and the same fiddler, lasted until dawn, with the fiddler occasionally singing "The Maid of Monterey" and "The Destruction of Sennacherib."

The only thing that made Noah sore was the way in which people who had brought the least provender were the greediest in carrying home the scraps—whole quarters of beef and the like.

Noah hadn't much use either for moochers or the utterly shiftless. He agreed with one of his neighbors who often said, "The Bible says, 'He that provideth not for his household is wuss'n an infidel.' "

Though Noah provided for his household, he still found time for and enjoyed hunting. But he and the Indians found deer much easier to stalk than turkeys. Noah liked to quote an Indian acquaintance who said, "Turkey hard to kill. Injun crawl in grass; deer, he says, 'Maybe so Injun; maybe so stump,' and then he go on and eat. Injun crawl a little closer and shoot him. . . . Turkey look and he say, 'Injun, by God!' and he duck his head and run."

Sometimes, seeing a herd of wild turkeys feeding on the prairie, Indians would chase them on horseback, sprinting under the flight until the exhausted turkeys fell to the ground. Then the Indians would lasso them. They also lassoed deer and wild horses by waiting near a water hole until the thirsty animals would come and drink all the water they could hold. It was a simple matter then to run them down and rope them. Mustang horses were sometimes captured by creasing their necks in a delicate way with bullets. Momentarily stunned, they were easily captured, but usually if hit at all they just died. Buffalo calves were got by driving the herd until the calves tired, fell behind, and were caught.

What chiefly irked the Indians was the white man's wanton destruction of the buffalo, sometimes for the hides, as often for sport. One of these buffalo hunters, eager for an instantly killing gun, asked Noah to bore out his gun barrel until the bullets would weigh eight to the pound. Noah complied, and when the hunter next took aim on a buffalo and pulled the trigger, the recoil dislocated his shoulder.

Noah himself was something of a bear hunter. Frequently when his dogs had a bear surrounded and he was afraid to shoot the bear for fear of hitting one of his dogs, Noah waded into the melee and, with a hunting knife, cut the bear's throat.

The most violent and paralyzing fright he ever got was given him by none of the charging buffalo bulls, which sometimes treed him, but occurred one night when he was lost in the Brazos River bottoms and was stalked by a panther which, when Noah was almost ready to die of terror, turned out to be a polecat. Only on this and one other occasion were Noah's emotions so uncontrollable that he broke down and cried. The other time was when, on the day Texas entered the union, he saw the Lone Star flag hauled down from above the capitol. Yet even on this occasion he managed to pull himself together well enough to give a reasonably sincere Texas yell when the Stars and Stripes went up in its place.

But all this time Noah was growing no younger—and now another and, to Noah, a sickening war was impending: the war between the North and the South. In the first place, Noah believed, like his idol, Andy Jackson, that the Union must be preserved. Secondly, he knew the South couldn't win—that the great cost of such a war would buy them nothing.

In the beginning Noah tried to urge his friends privately to help maintain the peace, but they wanted war.

When it was said one Southerner could lick ten Yanks, Noah, whose fighting reputation gave weight to his words, said that the Northerners had always fought well, and "when you parcel them out, you needn't give me but one, and I don't care to have him a very stout one."

Finally, in the face of violent hostility, Noah took the stump for peace, but it did no good.

Then he went to see Sam Houston, whom he loved.

"General," he said, wanting to detach Texas from the secessionist group, "if you'll unfurl the Lone Star from the capitol, I'll bring 100 men to help maintain it there."

But Houston said no. "I have done all I can to keep her from seceding," he said. "Now if she won't go with me, I'll have to turn and go with her."

So old Noah, who was salty when he got here, still had the spunk to brave the Apaches and deserts between himself and California rather then bend before what to him was a great mass evil.

"California will secede before you get there," one man said.

"Well if it does," Noah said, "I'll go on to the Sandwich Islands."

With that, Noah Smithwick—who had fought for Texas' revolution against Mexico, lived through and enjoyed her evolution from a wilderness to a full-fledged member of the Union, and who had loved Texas deeply—now abandoned his property, loaded his wagon and his rifle, and headed west.

15. As It Was in the Beginning

1

$\mathcal{I}$N THE halls of learning in my home town, there was, among others, one outstanding thing that I could never understand. Why was it, I wondered, that the histories of Greece and Egypt, of Europe and the United States, were to me engrossing, while that of Texas was dust and straw?

May God forgive me, but only after first forgiving the author of that textbook, who needs it, I cannot help feeling, even worse than I do. If ever this earth was trod by a more fascinating, endlessly intriguing man than Sam Houston, who was, as it were, the old stud possum of Texas history, I am unaware of that man's story. What other man combines in his nature the oratory of Demosthenes, the courage of Sergeant York, the intuition of Adolf Hitler, the personal magnetism of Winston Churchill, and the inexpressibly piquant and delightful theatrical ham of W. C. Fields?

Houston, however, was not the man who initiated that sequence of alarums and conflicts that marked the beginning of the Texas story. It was Stephen Austin, one of the few calm spirits whom Texas ever deigned to follow. Which immediately raises the point: if he was so calm and sane, what was he doing in Texas at that time?

In a sense he had Texas unloaded on him by his father, who was a well-intentioned but neither a very practical nor a discreet man. Yet except for certain anterior circumstances, Stephen's father would never have been granted permission to bring North American settlers into Texas—which was the thing that got Stephen implicated in this stormy narrative.

About a hundred years earlier, in what might be approximately described as the salad days of the eighteenth century, the King of Spain and the Pope, both eager to secure the allegiance of this vast domain that the Indians called "Tejas," had sent parties of soldiers and priests out to strategic points in this colony to build fortress-churches. And from said bases of operations, these ambassadors of King and Pope were to teach the Texas Indians that God was in heaven and by no means amused by all the scalping and butchery in which they indulged, or with their periodic raids into Mexico itself.

These fortress-churches were extremely impressive strongholds and—so far as the structures themselves went—impregnable. But the human beings who were to maintain these fountainheads of Christian civilization were less completely dedicated to the interests of King and Pope.

As a matter of fact, these workers-in-the-vineyard-abroad had largely been selected on a basis of the joy their absence would occasion at home. Almost all of the soldiery had resided, prior to their departure, in the various jails of New Spain, as Mexico was called at the time. And it was chiefly the human weakness of these fellows for Indian horses and maidens that, soon after the aforementioned missions were built, caused the Indians to hustle these soldiers, along with their ecclesiastical colleagues, on to the heavenly rewards they had originally come to advertise.

In a word, though it might be pleasant to hold title to so much land, the Spaniards were finding that the job of civilizing, developing, and administering it was more, by a good deal, than a nuisance.

But the Indians were not alone in giving offense to the Spanish colonial government. The French over in Louisiana, with a far greater knack for getting along with the Indians, were taking a big share of the commercial gravy that the territory afforded. Finally, ever so often, a band of impetuous North Americans would breeze into Texas and try to take the place over by force of arms. And while these little invasions never amounted to much, since the Spanish armies usually killed these people or chased them off, they were, nevertheless, an expensive annoyance.

So when old Moses Austin came along and promised to settle the place peacefully with North American families, each of which would pledge allegiance to Spain, join the Catholic Church, and slay its quota of Indians, the somewhat weary Spaniards could not find it in their hearts to refuse.

So far so good. But then old Moses, true to past performance (he was always starting things without finishing them), got lost on his way home, and subsisted so long on a diet of Texas air and sticks that when he got home, his splinter-riddled old mortal envelope collapsed, and he passed on to Abraham's bosom.

But not without leaving all sorts of death-bed messages to son Stephen to carry out his, Moses', great dream of "redeeming Texas from the wilderness."

So at this point young Stephen enters the story, and begins being, as he was subsequently dubbed, "the father of Texas." And that Texas' father should have lived and died in complete innocence of all matrimonial attachment was not, I suppose, in any sense out of character.

2

It is possible that when Stephen Austin was a child, the other children were occasionally rather baffled by certain more or less glacial facets of his personality. Seldom, perhaps never, did he do anything impulsively.

He was a handsome, thoughtful child with deep clear blue eyes and dark curly hair, to whom the whole rather helter-skelter character of his family life, dominated as it was by his father, must have been distasteful.

Stephen had a moderate flair for reading, but a far greater one for thinking and for orderly procedure. And after a little formal study in Connecticut and Kentucky, he was quickly recognized as being "sound" by his neighbors, who sent him to the Missouri legislature. But Stephen's spiritual home was in the orderly temples of the law, where logic and a kind of patrician justice that meant something to Stephen should prevail.

It must, therefore, have been with a kind of sickness of heart that Stephen came to grips with this residual confusion of his father's life: his father's unfulfilled obligation to colonize Texas.

More or less concurrently with the death of Stephen's father, the Mexicans had revolted and won their independence from Spain. It was necessary therefore for Stephen to go to Mexico City and make sure that the *permiso* his father had received from the Spaniards still held good.

This, in the early 1820's, he did, simultaneously acquainting himself with the mores of the Mexican politicos and discovering that the processes of Mexican law were interminable and almost inexplicable. But he also found that the Mexicans responded warmly to his personal dignity, calm elegance, and tact. They wanted him to take as much authority as he would over his colonists, so that their problems would not intrude themselves upon the Mexican government. Only cases of murder and the grandest larceny were to be referred to the Mexican courts. The other duties of government Stephen was to execute according to his discretion. The government did, however, take the trouble to decide that each family of settlers should gratuitously receive about four thousand acres of land.

At once, Stephen set about establishing his first settlers, carefully surveying and recording the land selected by each, and seeing that each got his share of river frontage and other emoluments. Meanwhile he carried on a colossal correspondence with the officials in Mexico City, with prospective settlers, and with relatives whom he had not yet persuaded to come.

To prospective settlers Stephen stressed the future more than the present. Otherwise he would have had to say something like this:

DEAR SIR:

If you come on to Texas by land from New Orleans, you will cross the most hideous swamps imaginable. If you come by sea, there is the possibility of being taken by the vessels of M. Jean Lafitte, a pirate, most strategically located on Galveston Island. If by chance you manage to get here, the savages will no doubt overtake you and destroy you.

As to the aspects of civilization in this new country, there is a

town in the northeastern part called Nacogdoches which, if you
come by land, will certainly be your first stop. It is inhabited
almost exclusively by criminals, the dregs of two civilizations.
Much farther south and west, however, is our metropolis, a
place called San Antonio de Bexar, containing several church-
fortresses, a number of soldiers, and the chief political representative of the Mexican government. In all, this leading city of
ours contains near one thousand souls, a large portion of which
are sorely in want of a square meal. The garrison troops, chroni-
cally unpaid, subsist by thieving from the poverty-stricken
civilians. Still farther south and nearer the coast are one or two
more villages. What lies to the westward, besides the most
bloody and incorrigible savages, only God and the rattlesnakes
know.

It is however true that the land in my colony is good and
plentiful. Compared to most of that east of the Appalachians, it
is an unbelievable paradise of fecundity. Moreover, wild game
abounds here: turkey, deer, buffalo, and horses—a wide selection
of the latter being available at around two dollars per head. I
list them as game because many of us have at certain places and
seasons found it necessary to rely on them for food.

As yet there is only one road worth mentioning in this entire
domain. It is a wagon track running from Nacogdoches through
San Antonio to Mexico City, a distance of about two thousand
miles. Otherwise one simply travels along the rivers as best one
can.

Furthermore, while I am making an almost superhuman effort
to select as settlers only the best element of society, there comes
this way an almost unstemmable tide of criminals and what
might roughly be called wild men.

We are totally without government except for my personal
offices. I travel constantly, surveying and recording the settlers'
head rights, trying cases of all kinds solely on a basis of my own
judgment. Yet it is simply a job that's got to be done. And I have
no choice but to trust my own judgment and instincts and go on
with it.

Ultimately, there is the problem of the questionable stability of the government that has granted this land to me for settlement. It is a despotism that the times have outmoded. Iturbide, the first Mexican ruler, has declared himself emperor, yet the Mexican people begin to catch the spirit of the French and American revolutions.

You can see, therefore, that if you come to this country and strive to carve a home out of the wilderness, your only protection and security in the future will be my ability to ride out these impending political storms, turning each of them to your advantage as one of my settlers. And I, alas, am but a quite young and inexperienced man.

It is therefore clear that your best interests will be served in staying wherever you are, even though by doing so you will be depriving me of the fee of twelve and a half cents per acre I would get for surveying and settling you on your land.

Sincerely yours,

STEPHEN F. AUSTIN

That is a letter Stephen Austin never wrote. In the beginning he had decided to subdue this wilderness and make it fruitful. That became the ultimate loyalty of his life. And though he was fundamentally a man of integrity, he never permitted himself to be guided by his more abstract loyalties at the expense of the cause to which he had dedicated himself.

Instead he wrote of Texas' shining future, of the sterling character of his colonists, which actually was far more palatable than that of the settlers outside it— particularly the hearties of the Red Lands in Northeast Texas.

In this latter region was truly the scum of the continent. It was they who gave the phrase "Gone to Texas" its additional meaning of having left in the middle of a dark night shortly before the arrival of the sheriff. Because of the scarcity of small coin, it was customary at this time in Texas to chop a silver dollar into eight pie-slices called "bits" and worth twelve and a half cents. In the Red Lands however, the dollars were beat out to a considerably increased circumference and then cut into ten or twelve bits. Counterfeiting paper money was also followed by many of the white-collar class, who left murder and robbery to those with less sedentary inclinations. Among the latter, a cowhide quirt was looked upon as far less distinguished and tony than one that had been plaited from the skin off a squaw's belly. In the production of these trinkets, plaiting began of course at the navel.

Yet despite these outlaw neighbors to the eastward and the savages to the west, Austin's colony grew and, in a certain threadbare sense, prospered.

But more troubling to Austin than either the savages or the population of the Red Lands were certain ardent spirits among his own people who had an implacable itch to drive the Mexicans out of Texas and seize it for themselves.

But by superhuman exertions Stephen Austin managed to keep his people at least semi-calm, and uninvolved in the no doubt inviting, certainly perpetual, convolutions and spasms of Mexican politics. Meanwhile tactfully, tirelessly, he struggled to gain state government for Texas, on an equal footing with the other states of the Mexican republic, and to talk away the Mexican government's dawning realization of the contempt in which the Texans held them.

For though the Texans had vowed allegiance to the Mexican government, they'd kept their fingers crossed, just as they had when they'd joined the Catholic Church.

And the war party in Texas, headed by the Brothers Wharton and such fire-eaters as William Barret Travis, continued to grow in importance and strength.

3

Since debarrassing itself of the Spanish rule, Mexico had treated itself to one revolution after another, in each of which a certain young Mexican militarist was having an increasingly important part. His name, for he was not yet known as the Napoleon of the West, was Antonio López de Santa Anna.

About the time Stephen Austin was establishing his colony, Santa Anna, at the age of twenty-six, had already had ten and a half years of army service, having been engaged in and schooled by the bloodiest, most brutal conflicts with assorted rebels and Indians. But not until a little later did Santa Anna pull off one of the most deft, yet most characteristic maneuvers of his career.

On February 24, 1821, General Iturbide pronounced his manifesto in favor of an independent Mexico, and Santa Anna, an officer in the colonial army of the King of Spain, was sent to exterminate the now massing patriots. He encountered them at Orizaba, where, on March 23, the rebels invited Santa Anna to join forces with them. At this suggestion he opened fire on them. And in the following few days he killed most of the revolutionists, and captured the rest, along with their arms and stores. His victory over the rebels was bloody and complete. At two o'clock, on the day of the victory, he joined the rebellion!

Prior to this *volte-face*, however, he had sent a report of his victory to his loyalist superiors. One of his demands on joining the rebels was a promotion of one full rank. Now word came that the Spanish viceroy had elevated him to the rank of lieutenant colonel for his good work in defeating the rebels. Santa Anna then made the rebels top that. Thus he'd wangled two promotions in one day, betrayed the crown, joined his prisoners and, no doubt, left all hands a little dizzy.

Now, despite the bad start Santa Anna had earlier made (he'd had the embarrassing misfortune to get caught with his hand in the regimental till) he was a full colonel at twenty-seven.

At the end of a series of additional revolutions and deft betrayals of everybody who gave him the chance, Santa Anna eventually emerged as a full general and a five-alarm national hero.

Now all this time he had posed as a liberal. I say posed, because Santa Anna was a fairly smart, fast-talking, tough Mexican on the make, who made not only political hay but cash out of every revolution.

But until 1835, his record had given the appearance of quasi-consistency. At this time the landowners, ecclesiastics, and army were advocating a political formula called *centralism*, which involved an abolition of states' rights and a good many individual ones. Now it was plain that the money was behind this side, but it was just as plain that the people would back the other— and Santa Anna had a use for the people. So he plumped for what might be called the Popular Front. And by this strategem he drew Austin, the heretofore utterly noncommittal Austin, to his side. For while Austin was a sort of congenital Republican at heart, the states' rights aspect of the anti-centralism faction appealed to him, who was himself a state boss.

On the strength of Austin's recommendation, Texas supported the general for the presidency, and the general was elected. But for all Santa Anna's hints of rewards for Texas, none came. There were so few priests in the country that a Texan who was lucky enough to find himself a wife could not marry her. And for such a couple simply to jump the broomstick and propagate was against the laws of the land.

As a matter of fact, soon after his election, Santa Anna just told the vice-president of Mexico to take care of things and himself went back to his estate at Jalapa and devoted himself to cock fighting, while the vice-president, a spiritual forerunner of the New Deal, tried experiments that, in his case, wouldn't work.

Finally Austin, growing tired of all this neglect of his colony, advised the Texans to form a state government with or without the consent of Mexico. This, with an uncharacteristic lack of discretion, he did by letter from Mexico City. The letter was intercepted, and Austin jailed.

With Austin gone, the war party in Texas took over.

But their job of incitement to war was made easy by General Santa Anna himself when, by a *coup d'état*, he had himself made dictator of Mexico.

Now His Excellency had dropped the hat the Texans had been waiting for. They hadn't the slightest intention of letting themselves be dictated to by anybody. Even Austin, who'd finally got out of jail in Mexico City and returned to Texas, greeted his fellows in convention assembled with the opinion that there was no alternative but war.

But since a leading figure in the war which was now about to start has yet to make an entrance in this narrative, and since he can fittingly do so only with a twenty-one-trumpet tarrraaa, it is necessary, momentarily, to digress.

4

On December 1, 1832, a huge handsome man, with chestnut hair and what Washington Irving had previously noted as a grandiloquent manner, was encamped on the United States side of the Red River, which formed the northern boundary of the Mexican territory of Texas. At the moment he was without much funds and without high office. He was possessed, in fact, of little more than a bob-tailed horse named Jack, his own unquenchable ambition, and the most dramatic and exciting name in America: Sam Houston.

Sam's father, an inspector of the Virginia militia, had died when Sam was fourteen, and the family had removed to new land in Tennessee, which Sam, in conjunction with his brothers, was to farm. However, Sam spent most of the plowing seasons away from home in the company of the Cherokee Indians, where his own natural dignity, disinclination for toil, and a kind of sweet and mystic megalomania made him always welcome, and prompted the Cherokee chief, Oo-loo-te-ka (He-puts-the-drum-away), to adopt Sam as his son.

On these excursions, which might be of any length from a few months to a year or two, Sam hunted with the braves, made love to the girls, and immersed himself in the classics of two cultures: the great legends, chiefly religious, of the Indians, and whatever books he had managed to bring along—the only requirement being apparently that they stand in the heroic tradition.

A little later, Sam fought in the Indian wars (not however against his friends, the Cherokees) under Old Hickory and, by his bravery and personal charm, won the lifelong affection of Jackson. And afterwards, it was Jackson, acting as Houston's sponsor, who saw Sam elected to offices of increasing importance until he became the governor of Tennessee and the logical man to follow Jackson to the White House. For everywhere Houston went he promptly won the hearts of the people with his magnificant bearing and courtesy, and the genuine hugeness of spirit which none of his neighbors ever failed to sense. Besides, even at this early date, his legend, as soldier, lover, gentleman, drinker, high-powered politico, and wit, was not to be sneezed at. Then he married a prominent Tennessee girl who left him almost before the honeymoon ended.

Why? Nobody knew. And in the absence of real
information, rumor was substituted, and that rumor
was hideous. Mobs began to howl against Houston.
A few days after his bride had decamped, he wrote
a letter to the Tennessee senate, thanking the state
for its past generosity to him, but, as he put it, "delicately circumstanced as I am," he resigned the governorship, explained nothing, went back to the Indians and
got drunk.

Dejected and hurt, he toyed with the idea of abandon-
ing civilized life for all time, of organizing the various
warring tribes of Indians into a single powerful nation
and holding the west for the Indians under himself.
Meanwhile he took unto himself a beautiful Indian
wife, Tiana Rogers, and contended for the inalienable
sovereignty of the Cherokee Nation, which the United
States was prone to violate at will. But much of the
time The Raven, as Houston was known to the Indians,
devoted himself exclusively to the flowing bowl.
Finally, however, acting as ambassador for the Indians,
Houston went to Washington, and while there had
occasion to cane a Congressman when the latter pronounced himself above receiving a dueling challenge
from Houston.

And here Houston's career turned back toward daring,
away from the spiritual retreat which his return to the
Indians usually signified.

"I was dying out," Houston later said, "and had they
taken me before a justice of the peace and fined me ten
dollars it would have killed me."

Instead, wearing a magnificent new outfit of clothes bought for him by the President of the United States, Sam was tried by Congress itself.

The verdict of the House was that Houston should be reprimanded and fined the flattering sum of five hundred dollars.

That trial put him back on his feet. By means of it, Houston had crowded everything off the front pages but himself. Again the realization was thrust upon him that he was a man of destiny.

A little later then, with Jackson's blessing and consent, Houston headed southwest, and after a little time spent with his Indian wife, he proceeded toward Texas.

In Texas, however, Sam Houston, grown cagy by the wealth of misfortune his impetuosity had earned him in the past, played his cards very close to his plum-colored vest. He practiced law and courted with seemly mildness in Nacogdoches, until the war started. Meanwhile he had been a fellow-traveler of the war party, without himself making rash commitments. Not only had he everything to gain by war, but he had personal ties with the war party leaders, the ever-belligerent Whartons, that dated back to the old days in Tennessee.

When hostilities first started, the Texans, though aware of Sam's well-publicized military prowess, hadn't the immediate foresight to elect Houston their commander. Instead, because Austin had been a good civil administrator, they elected him commander-in-chief.

But where Austin had always had trouble enough with his frontiersmen in times of peace, he soon found that their peacetime demeanor was lamb-like and cherubic compared to their behavior once they had gone on the war path.

Even before Austin could take command, a few of his command-to-be impetuously attacked and defeated a superior Mexican force at Gonzales. Then, once he'd assumed command and revealed himself to be a council-of-war general, instead of a firm, self-confident commander, Austin's junior officers began to give advice that bordered on the insolent. Still worse, his incoming troops seemed to feel it a kind of duty to eat all the food, drink all the whisky and, whether their consolation were welcome or not, console all the women encountered en route.

Austin was helpless, baffled, and miserable. He advised the state convention then in session to select a military man for commander-in-chief, and to send him, Austin, as commissioner to the United States where, under less turbulent circumstances, he might raise men and money as well as political approbation for the Texans' cause.

In this fashion, then, matters were arranged. Austin was sent to the United States. Henry Smith was made governor. And Sam Houston was elected commander-in-chief of the armies.

5

While Houston at San Felipe set about devising a more orderly military establishment and ordering tomahawks and chewing tobacco for hoped-for Indian allies, he suggested to the army that it retire from its nominal siege of the Mexican garrison at San Antonio, furlough most of the men, and wait for artillery before attempting to assault the fortified city. The army, however, was bored and restless, tired of the rural scenery outside of San Antonio, when all the ladies and liquor, excitement and potential victory, were inside. Moreover, when it felt like fighting, the Texas army was not dependent on the approbation of some distant general sitting at a desk.

Austin had left Burleson in command until such time as Houston could arrive on the field. Burleson too realized the folly of attacking the fortifications with muskets. The army, nevertheless, could no longer be denied. And when one of their number inquired, "Who'll go into Bexar [San Antonio] with old Ben Milam?" 301 volunteered, and in the face of artillery fire stormed the town.

The victory which Houston had said couldn't happen did happen, and it was a mighty blow to his prestige.

Among the leaders in this battle had been a Dr. James Grant, whose mines below the Rio Grande had been confiscated by the Mexican government, and who sorely wanted them back.

Now as one of the Men-who-were-right, he began advocating an attack on the Mexican port of Matamoros. Once Matamoros was taken, the army would be in excellent position to recover Dr. Grant's property for him.

Houston and Governor Smith opposed the expedition; the General Council favored it—and an irreparable damage had been done to the Texas cause: the leadership was split and pulling in opposite directions.

In any case, Grant ran off with Houston's army and headed for Matamoros. Houston heard of it from Colonel Neill, who'd been left in San Antonio in an old fortress-church nicknamed the Alamo in command of eighty sick and wounded men whom Grant had stripped even of medicine.

At once Houston set out to try to overtake and stop his truant army. On January 14, 1836, Houston caught Grant, who now called himself "Acting Commander-in-chief," at Goliad. Grant had seized all the horses and supplies he could find, and his men were in high and aggressive spirits, ready to follow where Grant should lead.

Just here, to make matters worse, Houston heard from Neill that the Mexicans were marching on San Antonio. At once he sent Jim Bowie with a handful of men to instruct Colonel Neill to evacuate and destroy the Alamo.

And then the final blow fell. Word came that the General Council had deposed Smith as governor and Houston as commander-in-chief, in favor of Fannin. And Fannin, a Grant man, was determined to march on to Matamoros.

That broke Houston's spirit—temporarily. Filled with frustration and defeat, he followed his old formula of going back to the Indians. With these easy, unde-manding people he rested for a while, and renewed his grip upon himself, his interior poise, his will to attack and to win.

When he returned to the white man's world, he arrived with intuitive drama, just when the convention at Washington-on-the-Brazos was bogged down in a slough of disagreement, rain, mud, and leaderless defeat. News had come the day before that the Alamo (Houston's order for the evacuation had not been obeyed) was besieged and that the chances of defending it successfully were almost nonexistent. Already refugees were beginning the eastward march.

Houston's arrival created a sensation, and henceforth he dominated and inspired the convention. That night a Declaration of Independence was drawn up. It was approved March 2, Houston's forty-third birthday. The following day Houston was again elected commander-in-chief.

News from the Alamo was looking still worse. One delegate suggested the convention adjourn and go to relieve it. Houston demanded the legislators stay in session, and told them that he would deal with the enemy himself.

With his aide, Major Hockley, and three volunteers, one in a borrowed suit of clothes, the Commander-in-chief went forth to face General Santa Anna and his army of 6,000 men.

When Houston reached Gonzales on March 11, he found 374 men under Moseley Baker. They had food for two days and three cannon, one of which was being patched up in a blacksmith shop.

Hardly however had Houston started to form the men into companies, when word arrived that the Alamo had fallen. At once Houston had the Mexicans who had brought this news arrested as harbingers of false rumor, in an effort to quell some of the hysteria that their tidings had caused.

Now he set about to organize his men, whose number in two days had grown to 500, into a regiment under Burleson with an order to start drill and establish discipline against that time when the shattering news of the Alamo could be no longer suppressed. Soon three of the non-combatant survivors arrived and pandemonium broke loose among the town and the army. But Houston laid a hard hand upon them and held them, all but twenty, who got away and spread their tale of horror. At once Houston sank his artillery in the river, burned whatever else he could not move, and the retreat of the army began.

Meanwhile a detachment of Mexican dragoons had overtaken Grant's party (which had split off from the army under Fannin) and annihilated them. The Texas government had flown to Harrisburg. Civilians, both in company with the army and on their own, were fleeing with what they could carry. Only by marching his army to the point of absolute exhaustion, was Houston able to maintain any semblance of order and prevent rout. But as the army retreated through the less sparsely settled lands, Houston's avowed determination to fight and promises of victory drew recruits to the army until its number reached 1,400.

But Houston was not yet ready to fight. His whole strategy, as he had previously written to a friend, was to retreat with such diligence that Santa Anna would divide his forces in an effort to hem the Texans in a pocket. Houston's plan was then to fall upon these separate forces and destroy them. As the retreat continued, the news came on March 25 that Fannin, in command of the only other considerable force of Texas soldiers, had been attacked by one of Santa Anna's wing columns at Goliad and defeated.

Houston drove his army on in headlong retreat. The government, the people, his soldiers, begged him to stand and fight. Without explanation he continued the retreat.

On March 31, 1836, only 900 dispirited and rebellious men remained of the 1,400 that had retreated from the Colorado five days before. The country, like the army, was fast losing confidence in Houston.

Now another demoralizing blow fell. It was learned that Fannin and the 390 men with whom he had surrendered at Goliad had been massacred while held as prisoners of war. Horror gripped Texas more tightly.

The Runaway Scrape, as the flight of the colonists' families was called, grew in scope and pace. Only Sam Houston's frustrated and mutinous mob remained to face the four Mexican columns dashing forward to encircle it.

As the Texas army proceeded eastward, suspense in

the ranks was growing unbearable. Was Houston going to lead the army on into the United States or would he try to intercept Santa Anna at Harrisburg?

When the crossroads were reached, some of the troops favored flight across the Sabine. Ignoring this chatter, the general sent his advance guard over the Harrisburg road.

Despite the fact that several hundred of Houston's men left him at this crossroad, he set out to track down Santa Anna, to find and attack him before his wing columns could come to his assistance.

Santa Anna had reached and destroyed Harrisburg (the Texas government had already fled to Galveston Island) and passed on before Houston got there. Nevertheless the trail was growing hot, the quarry near.

Next day Houston harangued his men. "Victory is certain!" he said. "Trust in God and fear not! And remember the Alamo! Remember the Alamo!"

"Remember the Alamo!" the men shouted back. "Remember Goliad!" Now they had a battle cry.

The stage was set for the Battle for Texas.

On the night preceding its first phase, Houston had his men slithering through the woods, ferrying bayous, and performing other such stealthy maneuvers. Yet when morning came, there was an entirely formal and largely inconsequential artillery duel between Houston's two cannon and one of Santa Anna's. There was also an exchange of musket fire.

During this skirmish Santa Anna's cannon was damaged, and then withdrawn. And Houston, though time was on Santa Anna's side, did not press this advantage.

Instead, he fiddled about until night came, and then had himself a fine sleep—the longest since the retreat began.

What possessed the man?

He knew reinforcements were en route to Santa Anna's camp. As a matter of fact, 600 men under General Cos arrived that very night. Could Houston conceivably have hoped to surprise Santa Anna on the morrow, the very next day after their artillery duel? Or was this hesitation the result of the plain indecision of a mind beclouded by the mysticism of the Indians, and of a temperament that could never act with complete certainty except by intuition?

In any case, on the day after this inviting opportunity had been passed up, Houston called a council of war, heard the opinions of his officers, and sent them away. From then until three-thirty he brooded. Then he ordered his army to form for the attack.

At four he drew his sword and raised it over his head. A drum and fife struck up "Come to the Bower," and the last 800 fighting men who stood between Texas and annihilation started slowly across the plain of San Jacinto, protected by a swamp on their left and on their right by two good cannon, Millard's forty-eight regulars and Mirabeau Buonaparte Lamar's fifty cavalrymen. Houston, on a white stud horse, rode up and down the front, calling to his men to hold their fire, knowing that action now must be decisive and final.

For ten minutes the single line moved through the thigh-high grass. Before it was a barricade of Mexican camp equipment. In the Mexican camp a bugle split the air. A few bursts of musketry came from behind the Mexican breastworks. Several Texans raised their rifles and replied.

"Hold your fire!" Houston shouted. "God damn you, hold your fire!"

The white stallion fell and Houston, taking a cavalry man's horse, continued patrolling his line. Deaf Smith, Houston's ace scout, rode up. "Fight for your lives!" he yelled. "Vince's Bridge has been cut down!"

In the minds of the Texans, that meant all retreat was cut off.

Twenty paces from the barricade Houston gave a signal with his hat. A charge from his cannon flattened a section of the breastwork. The infantry let go a volley and ran forward with drawn hunting knives, yelling, "Remember the Alamo! Remember Goliad!"

On they swept over the battered barricade. The Mexicans tried to form in companies and platoons, firing and running back. But, however unbelievable it might seem, the Mexicans were totally "surprised." Santa Anna, beguiled by too much success, never dreaming that Houston with his inferior force would dare attack, was having a siesta in his marquee. Cos's men, who'd marched throughout the preceding night, were also asleep. Cavalrymen were riding their unsaddled horses back from the watering place. Some were cooking and cutting wood. Most of the Mexican rifles remained stacked. A Mexican general rallied a few men to a field piece, but before it could go into action, the gun crew was cut down by the Texans' knives. General Almonte, Santa Anna's chief to staff, rounded up 400 men and managed to get them away. Rushing from his tent, Santa Anna viewed the panic, shouted a few unheard orders, then leaped on the first horse he could catch and fled.

By now the Texas army was entirely out of control. They were a mob dealing with a fallen enemy from which they had for so long been fleeing. Clubbing, knifing, shooting, they butchered the Mexicans where they found them. One group of Texans, finding a detachment of cavalry forming, drove them over the embankment where Vince's Bridge had been, and the clutching men and pawing horses drowned together.

As the afternoon grew late, Houston, astride his third horse, his right boot full of blood (a ball had shattered the bone just above his ankle), saw a column of Mexican infantry approaching and his heart sank. His own men were scattered, killing what Mexicans they could find. The approaching force were visibly veterans. But the suspense was not long-lived. The column was headed by General Almonte, coming forward to surrender his 400 men.

As night fell and the casualties were counted, it was learned that six Texans were killed and twenty-four wounded. The Mexicans had lost some 500 killed, 200 wounded, and about 600 prisoners. The battle, as such, had lasted about twenty minutes. The butchery went on into the night. But when the surviving prisoners were herded into a circle, Santa Anna was not to be found.

On the evening of the following day Houston, despite his night of pain, had fashioned a little garland of leaves (such occasions always brought out the ham— but sweet and toothsome—in Houston) and inscribed a card to his girl of the moment which said, "To Miss Anna Raguet, Nacogdoches, Texas. These are laurels I send you from the battle of San Jacinto. Thine Houston."

A little later then, a patrol rode into camp bringing with it a profoundly sad Mexican in a blue cotton smock and red felt slippers. He'd been found near the old Vince's Bridge head, sitting on a stump in despair. But as this scrap of broken spirit and printed cloth entered the camp, the Mexican prisoners began to uncover their heads and exclaim, "*El presidente!*"

Seeing now that he was recognized, the dejected man asked to see General Houston. This was granted.

Houston was lying on a blanket under a tree. The Mexican stepped up to him, bowed in a way that was devoid of arrogance but not of grace, and said in Spanish, "I am General Antonio López de Santa Anna, president of Mexico, commander-in-chief of the army of operations. I place myself at the disposal of the brave General Houston."

Houston raised himself on one elbow. "General Santa Anna! Ah, indeed! Take a seat, General. I'm glad to see you. Take a seat."

Houston's man, Zavala, came forward to act as interpreter. Santa Anna pointed out that it would

hardly be cricket for Houston to treat so distinguished
a prisoner as himself with anything less than the com-
pletest consideration; a point of view which Houston
said baffled him since Santa Anna had systematically
slaughtered every prisoner he took. This broke the
suave Santa Anna's stride. He became fussed and frightened, said he didn't feel well, asked for and received a
piece of opium, which gave him a much needed lift.
When Santa Anna sought to discuss peace terms,
Houston declined, saying that such matters were outside
his province and within those of the civil government.
Houston did, however, agree to an armistice, the terms
of which were drawn up. These included the immediate
removal of the remaining Mexican armies on Texan
soil, and instructions to this effect were sent at once by
Deaf Smith to the commanders of Santa Anna's other
columns which had not arrived in time for the battle.

And though even now gangrene was taking the meas-
ure of Sam Houston, and the Texas volunteers were
entertaining themselves by discussing novel ways in
which to dispatch Santa Anna, the Battle of Texas had
been fought and won.

6

At the news of Santa Anna's capture at San Jacinto,
America was first incredulous then joyous. Houston
went to New Orleans for repairs to his person. The
acclaim he received there was wild and soothingly
worshipful. But long before his cure was completed,
Houston heard of the political upheaval in Texas and

started back. To rest on his achievements now would have been a mistake that Houston had no intention of making. Besides, somebody had to look after Santa Anna. Alive, he was worth his weight in diamonds to Texas as a bargaining lever. If the impulsive population got hold of him, he would immediately become just another dead Mexican.

When the time came for the first post-victory elections, Houston's name was presented as a candidate for president of the Republic. Eleven days before the test at the polls he consented to run, his stated reason: "The crisis requires it." He was, of course, elected by a huge majority, despite the fact that the other candidates were Austin and ex-Governor Smith. A constituency that was short on memory and long on enthusiasm, a constituency that had elected Austin, a statesman, the first military commander-in-chief, now named Houston, a military man of credit, its president.

For at the same time Sam Houston was conquering the Mexican army, he was also conquering the affections, and imaginations of Texans, then and forever.

16. Texas At War

1

I LEFT home at four o'clock that morning and went downtown. It was cold. A norther had sprung up earlier in the night and the temperature had dropped thirty degrees. It now stood at eighteen and the wind sliced through my clothes as if I hadn't any on.

As I passed the all-night cafe where ordinarily two or three people would have been, I saw through the sweat-dimmed glass doors fifteen or so men.

Then I saw the waiting busses, four of them—big ones, interior lights burning—lined up before the City Hall. Lights were also burning upstairs in the City Hall.

I had a sense of *déjà vu*, of having experienced this scene before. Then I remembered. It was in the Spanish Civil War. The lorries loaded with men going to the front. The whole thing was there, out of my book memory, out of *Man's Hope*, out of Hemingway.

I went into the cafe and ordered a cup of coffee. Among the group around the stove were the drivers of the four busses. Near me on a stool sat a youth in a brown suit. He was just sitting there, wishing the time would pass, that five o'clock would come.

"You going?" I asked.

He said he was.

"Had any sleep?" I asked.

"No."

The town night watchman came in shivering.

"Let's go out to my car and have a drink," I said. I thought we all needed it. I'd been working all night.

Outside, three whopping drinks killed the half-bottle. The night watchman went back into the cafe. The young man and I drove around the town, up on the hill. I drove past a house where a friend of mine who was going was spending the night. Inside the house a light was burning, but nobody could be seen. We drove on back to the City Hall, stopped the car, and went in.

There on the long wide stairway were the men who were leaving. I went on upstairs and leaned against a wall, hearing them talk (there was not much talk), looking at them. I was astonished by the absence of tension, the lack of fear among them, as they were about to plunge into a life that was wholly foreign to them. They were not even nervous enough to be talkative, though most of them had had a sleepless night in which to think. They just stood around.

As I looked at them, I knew I was seeing what American democracy and Texas were. I understood better what had happened at the Alamo. This appalling ease of casual fellowship, the almost visible comfort each man drew from the presence of the rest.

Here were boys I'd never seen before in my life, boys that the backwoods had disgorged. How many thousands of miles of furrow had this group plowed, how many hundred cords of wood had it cut?

Near me, in great splendor, stood a man, twenty-eight or thirty, who was obviously a citizen of Virginia City in another era. His hat was black and big. His suit fit with a kind of intentional tightness; his black shirt had white tasseled lacings instead of buttons; the pockets were edged in white, the piping ending in embroidered arrowheads. His sideburns were three inches long, extending forward in points toward his nose. His moustache was precisely in keeping with the rest. Yet his face was not without character. I felt sure he'd make a good soldier.

Near by was a youth in thin, blue, cotton breeches, a light, cheap, un-warm jumper, an old straw work hat. This was January, remember, and cold. His clothes were the worst there and I knew he was ashamed of them, that their shameful cheapness was more important to him than that they didn't keep him warm. And yet he didn't shrink away. He stood straight among the others, and I doubted if he'd ever be called upon for a greater display of guts. I liked him and silently wished him well.

Most of the other boys' clothes were cheap. Most didn't have suits. A majority of those that did had eleven-dollar suits from Sears and Roebuck. Most of them looked as if they didn't know too much about the war. Chiefly they looked like boys not keenly informed, but boys you'd like to soldier with, boys with a kind of countrified hardihood and dependability.

I saw the town tough-nut. I thought he'd make a fair soldier. I saw the town ne'er-do-well, thief, drunkard, knife fighter, swindler and liar. I thought he would make a bad soldier. I knew what his name would have been at the Alamo. There were dozens of gentler boys whom he might have thought of as sissies whom I'd rather have stand back to back with me in a fight.

What were these boys here for? Because they'd been told to come. In the main, there was no question about that. A few, of course, had wanted to go earlier, but had family obligations, perhaps to help an aging father make a crop. But now the choice was no longer theirs to make.

A few steps away from me was a Mexican father, full of quiet, peasant dignity and sorrow, a man whom fifty years had used hard, but a man in whom many days of hard labor were left. His big face was completely immobile. It was beautiful. I knew Orozco would have found it inspiring. Which was his son? The father stood alone.

All of the Mexican boys looked good. They looked healthy and intelligent. Those in whom the Indian strain was most visible were magnificent. Hardships that would break most men would not destroy these Mexican-Indian lads. Some people, forgetting the fighting qualities of the Spaniards and the Indians, might minimize these boys. I was thankful they weren't our enemies.

Across the hall was an old German with his baby. I knew the lad beside him was the old man's baby, the last child he could have bred. They never spoke to each other because they would not have known what to say. The little old man had pink-and-white cheeks, round eyes, a white handle-bar moustache. His son, the only frightened boy there, had obviously grown up close to the family hearth somewhere deep in the country. Like his father he was quite small. His little hat helped to make him look silly. His face ran forward on a more or less even plane from his occasionally moving Adam's apple to his bulging, quivering eyes. The expression on his face was one of deferential attention to this simple, but to him obviously confusing, scene. If anyone bumped his arm, the brushing touch shocked him hard inside. Quickly, brittlely, uncomprehendingly, he'd smile, without moving, never leaving his father's side, holding on, inside himself, to his father's presence.

I hoped to God the Army would reject this boy.

My friend came up the stairs with his wife. He had just started in business, and when his call came, he was being promoted by his company. As they came up the steps, the wife, a painfully shy girl, smiled brightly and bravely at the men along the stairs. She didn't speak to anybody because she couldn't. She was, I knew, holding on to the earth with her toes, but she was holding on.

I asked my friend how he was feeling.

"Topnotch," he said.

I moved away. There was no use in doing a lot of talking.

A man came out of an office with a pad and pencil in his hand.

"All right, men," he said, "answer to your names and be assigned to busses."

He had a loud, solid voice and when he hit the newly established silence with those names, they spread like dumdum bullets—good Texas names, fighting names.

"Jim Ferguson Clampett!"

"Here."

"Bus Number One.

"Sam Houston Cummings!"

"Here."

"Bus Number One."

"Joe Bailey Jones!" "Sam Bass Richardson!" "Barret Travis Simms!"

More and more names. Down the steps they went as their names were called. Down they went in their big hats, cowboy boots, cheap suits. A college boy in an expensive tweed went down grinning and hitting the steps with hard heels. Now the ragged boy started down at a brisk clip. Out of nowhere a strange *Gemütlichkeit* was arising. Everything was beginning to seem wonderful to everybody. A sudden unstated pride in themselves had struck these boys.

Another name was read. A big boy near me answered and turned to his father and mother. Quietly his mother kissed him.

"Coming to the bus?" the boy asked his father.

His father took his hand. "No son. Good-by."

Another set of heels hit the steps.

I noticed three women downstairs at the open door. They'd been standing there three-quarters of an hour and must have been frozen. Besides, they weren't dressed very well. Plainly one was a mother, the other a little sister, the third a wife—quite soon to be a mother herself.

I went down and told them there was a stove upstairs.

"No," the older woman said, "if we went up there, we couldn't see our boy leave."

The first bus was nearly full now.

From upstairs I heard my friend's name called. A moment later he was in his bus. His wife quickly vanished in the dark.

In half an hour the busses were loaded. A sign was given, and the interior lights were switched out.

One by one, quiet and dark, the busses pulled out, heading for San Antonio.

Still the town was asleep. In an hour or so, most of the people would be awake, but most of them would not understand how much, in this one night, the town had aged.

2

It stood to reason there was going to be trouble when the Army Air Force moved into Victoria, Texas. Because Victoria is by no means an ordinary town.

One look at the cowmen squatting on their heels outside its Manhattan Cafe would convince you there was not thirty-five dollars cash money in the crowd. Their clothes are coarse and cheap, their high-heeled boots scuffed by briars and stained grey-green by dung. But if those same men should jot down their net assets on a pad, the total would run between seventy-five and a hundred million dollars.

For Victoria is the ancestral seat of such great land and cattle baronies as those of the O'Connors, the Welders, the Keerans, the McFaddins. Among its 12,000 citizens are two dozen millionaires, living in fine big comfortable homes, surrounded by lovely lawns and gardens. To these people, whose ranches stretch as far as a hundred miles away, the town itself represents not a field of commercial adventure, but home—which they built to suit themselves.

Land and cattle are, in their opinion, the only really interesting and important kinds of property. Ranching, to them, is a mixture of business, sport, and religion—the only remaining way in which a free, proud man can earn entirely clean, hard money.

A few years ago some concern was felt by Victoria's grandees when the town was threatened by an oil boom. The boom actually came, but the large landowners got most of the money. Victoria, they found with a sigh of relief, was not to have its cow-town mores disturbed by this untoward mineral discovery. It was to be spared the bustle and general shabbiness of a boom town. And for fear somebody might think of them as oil men, the cattle men quietly, almost furtively, banked this new wealth and went about their old ways in their old clothes.

For in the scale of social prestige in Texas, oil money is, in comparison to that gained in cow ranching, worth about twelve or fifteen cents on the dollar.

Last summer Victoria was threatened again. Some of the small business people started a movement to bring an Army flying school to the town. Obviously there was nothing in it for the land and cattle barons except their great enemy: change. Too, a good many rumors had already reached Victoria about the trouble that its neighboring town of Palacios, fifty miles to the east, was having with the soldiers at Camp Hulen. Once the word went round that some white boys from the Bronx were going down the streets of Palacios with a Negro girl on each arm. Such reports as these were received by the men who squat on their heels outside the Manhattan with no talk at all, but were followed by seven or eight minutes of extremely fast whittling.

When it became more and more likely that a pursuit pilot school was actually coming to Victoria, the tempo of the whittling increased again.

What of the beauty of the town? Would it be filled with shabby barracks?

What of vice? Would the town be flooded with gamblers and whores? Would Dutch Lane, the town's small pre-war red light district, grow out of bounds?

Would it be safe for wives and daughters to go about unchaperoned at night?

Wouldn't this town become a changed, strident place entirely unlike that which the old hands had built and made beautiful and been happy in?

First these things were thought, then voiced. The people who'd profit from the air base were taking steps to hasten its arrival. A lot of other people, whose grand-daddies had killed an awful lot of Mexicans to make this land in their own image, were worrying.

Finally, the coming of the Army was a certainty. The group that wanted the training school had taken a 25-year lease on "a piece of country," as the ranch folk say, some 1,000 acres 5 miles east of town, and had offered it to the government at a rental of $1 per year. It was to be named Foster Field after a Texas flier killed in line of duty.

The pursuiters, the least conservative element of the least conservative branch of the Army, were moving into the most conservative town in Texas. For the great ranching families' whole identification is with the past rather than with the present or the future.

Soon Colonel Warren R. Carter, who was to command the new post, arrived with his staff. And those who met him, though disinclined to make hurried judgments, guardedly reported that he wasn't so bad. He was quiet, as they were quiet: a reserved, courteous gentleman, with sharp brown eyes, who was not going to try to put anything over on anybody, and it was plain that nobody was going to put anything over on him.

The Victorianos liked that. Besides, they soon found that Colonel Carter had been born up at Brownwood, Texas, and that helped too.

Next, when there was a place to put them, came the

Air Force ground crew to make arrangements to keep the pilots aloft when they should arrive later on.

These ground force lads turned out to be the kind of fellows whom some physical or educational deficiency had kept out of a cockpit, but who had elected to be just as near one as possible. They were men doing a job they knew was important, one in which they had been schooled and one they had mastered. Finally, this Air Force ground force world was a fast-expanding, boom world in which promotions and special ratings were showered on any man who could fill the bill. The Air Force needed thousands of non-commissioned officers to handle the spectacularly growing ranks, and it soon began to appear that there were as many men in Victoria with stripes on their sleeves as those without them.

These ground force people were, by Army standards, prosperous people, people with position, doing a job they liked. In a word, they were prideful people whom the Victorianos found astonishingly like themselves.

To house these noncoms and their families, a new addition was built onto the town and named Will Rogers Terrace. The houses were simple, comfortable, and in good taste. Nobody on either side had any right to resent them.

Meanwhile, the folks on both sides of the fence began to get acquainted. The brown bears and the black bears began to discover that they were all just bears together.

The town gave a party of welcome for this first contingent, and everything went off fine. The men received so many invitations for Sunday dinners that some of them did not taste Mess Hall fare on Sunday for months.

Since quarters were still somewhat scarce, Sergeant John Advent (twenty-three) and his pretty young wife Melba (twenty-two), both from Cleveland, moved into a small apartment house in town.

Because John's salary as a sergeant could stand a little reinforcement, Melba, who'd done stenographic work for H. J. ("57") Heinz in Cleveland, began looking for a job. Neither John nor Melba can yet understand how it happened, but two perfect strangers called up and gave Melba tips on possible jobs. But by that time, one of their co-tenants in the apartment house who was connected with the Texas Unemployment Commission had already got Melba a job at the Foster Field Hospital where she is still working.

Soon afterward Melba joined a little circle of young girls who met once a week to drink tea and discuss books. In this group Melba carries a great deal of weight because she is in such a splendid position to make dates for the other girls with soldiers.

Since there is as yet no special school for Army children, these youngsters go to the Victoria public schools, and their mamas join in with the Victoria mamas in running the Parent-teachers Association. All contribute to candy and bridge benefits. Not only do the soldiers' wives get along with the civilian wives, the Army wives, it is alleged, even manage to get along with each other, despite the variation in their husbands' rank.

That the single Air Force men are finding communion
with town girls is indicated by the fact that many of
Victoria's teachers and beauty parlor operators who
have never been outside of Texas are now accent special-
ists who can hear a soldier say two sentences and tell
him what state he comes from.

The first few soldiers who wandered into the Victoria
Presbyterian Church saw at once that its pastor, Sam
Hill, was a good preacher, but they must have wondered
if Sam would not have been better cast as the leader of a
band of guerrillas. For this loose-jointed, tow-headed,
six-foot-four preacher can knock a grown man through
a corral fence, ride anything with hair on it, and throw
any steer that ever walked. Rough country is his natural
element, a horse his natural means of locomotion. He's
hard and tough and intelligent—aggressive and a born
leader.

If an additional fillip of appeal were needed for Sam
Hill to captivate his cow-ranching, plane-flying congre-
gation (and it isn't needed), he could point to the ac-
complishments of his kid brother, "Tex," who flew with
the A.V.G. in Burma, and who had, at the last report,
shot down or destroyed on the ground the handsome
total of 58 Jap planes. For that matter, Sam's father, old
P. B. Hill, erstwhile missionary to Korea, now chaplain
to the Texas Rangers, is himself a man of distinction and
note in Texas.

But despite the fact that Sam's new khaki-clad com-
municants were getting to like him and Victoria, they
still looked forward to their Christmas leave.

At choir practice on the night of December 5, the boys were all talking about how they would get home. Jubilant discussions arose as to the relative merits of bus, train, or thumb. Everybody was in high and expectant spirits.

Two days later, of course, war began. And all leaves were canceled

One of Sam's parishioners, Mrs. Royston Nave, whose past philanthropies had chiefly been anonymous, decided to come out in the open and make a frontal attack on the disappointment among the men.

Mrs. Nave, incidentally, was originally a McFaddin, and is one of the principal stockholders in the McFaddin Estate, which Claude McCan, her son, operates, and which, counting land owned and leased, runs cattle over a piece of country comprising about a third of a million acres.

Mrs. Nave phoned Sam Hill, told him to run through the soldier's names in the church guest book and get word to the boys to come over to her house for a party. Sam got the boys, about ninety of them, and Mrs. Nave got the girls. And when the party was over, there wasn't a gloomy boy, or a hungry one, in the crowd.

As for young Sergeant John and Mrs. Advent, who'd also planned to get back to Cleveland and had never been away from home at Christmas before in their lives, every person they'd ever met in Victoria came to see them. People they hardly knew brought them presents. "Christmas," the Advents say, "went off swell."

And then, a little later on, the first class of cadets

breezed into town: all straight and young and somehow
bonny, the pride of a proud nation—and its best, if best
was to mean what it had always meant in Texas.

None of the early Texans who, armed with a so-so
legal case, a few muskets and butcher knives, had taken
Texas away from the Mexicans, had anything these boys
didn't have. What the proudest of the Victorianos had,
these youngsters could match. In such company it was
not really important who owned the most cows. And
the town turned out and took them to its heart.

When they reach Victoria, the pursuiters have
finished both their primary and basic training. At
primary the cadet's disposition was a little clouded by
the recurrent thought, "Six months from now I'll
probably be dead." During that time he had a tendency
to be somewhat desperate and extreme in his actions, to
drink too much when he got the chance, to talk too
loud. From primary he went to basic. Perhaps he took
his basic training at swank, hard-driving, spit-and-
polish Randolph Field. Here, working harder than he
ever had before, and under great pressure, he'd never
quite been able to relax in soldier-jammed San Antonio
on his one free day a week.

Then one day the class of 42-E awoke from this strain
and found itself in Victoria on the last lap of its training
course at Foster Field, where discipline is only nominal,
and the cadet's principal duties are to fly and fire, which,
to a pursuiter, is like getting money from home.

By now it was getting on toward spring. The mesquites were beginning to "green up," the scissor tails to

fly. The roadsides were striped with great pink ribbons of primroses, the pastures splotched red with Indian paintbrush. Elsewhere were yellow islands of wild daisies, thousands of acres of bluebonnets. And, as the cadet strolls across Victoria's square with a pretty girl on his arm, his new military personality begins to emerge.

That feeling of the touch of sudden death on his shoulders now has been assimilated because he is young and healthy, can adjust to anything and refuses to be perpetually gloomy. No longer does he worry about what will happen six months hence. He is easy and, in an entirely relaxed way, enjoys minutes and hours as they present themselves.

The feeling of this cow town for its heroes is one of almost shy affection and respect. Neither partner to this relationship has the lack of judgment to presume that he is dealing with his inferiors.

But this feeling is a gentle undertone rather than an overtone. There is no stiffness between these young sky-fighters and the Victorianos.

Usually the Victoria folk just invite the pursuiters to join in whatever they themselves enjoy doing. Maybe that is to go out to a cow camp and watch the ranch hands "load out" a train of cattle. For when one rancher loads out, his friends (men and women) are apt to gather at the loading pens to see what kind of cattle he's sending to market, to enjoy the exciting bustle, the yelling of the loaders—simply to gather in a setting that is meaningful and good to them because it is the harvest time in the ranching cycle.

Once the loading is done (a well-organized outfit will load a car with cattle in forty seconds), guests and cow hands go over to the chuckwagon and have a sound and succulent meal of camp bread, coffee, frijole beans and son-of-a-bitch stew.

Other Victorianos whose yachts and speed boats have not yet been confiscated by the Navy (the speed boats are used for crash boats at Naval air bases) take the boys down to the coast to cruise and swim, to fish for trout and mackerel and redfish.

On Sundays such housewives as Mrs. J. R. Gervais, about to leave for church, usually just tell the cook to name a number she can feed. At church then, Mrs. Gervais will recruit a gang of cadets and enlisted men, maybe even a lieutenant or two, and bring them home to eat and paw over the funny papers and probably hang around until it's time, in the interval between Jack Benny and Charlie McCarthy, to make a pot of coffee and go to work on the left-overs from dinner.

When Mr. J. A. Donaldson, an accountant whose hobby is photography, takes home a bunch of boys on Sunday, all hands take pictures, then develop them. While waiting for the prints to dry, they sometimes run home movies in the living room. When the pictures are finished, the boys usually mail some home.

The USO in Victoria also makes sense. It is adequately equipped with pool tables, ping-pong sets, basket-ball courts, writing, shaving, and shoe-shining equipment. Too, it has a well-equipped kitchen, so that any time the boys feel like cooking up a snack, all they've got to do is get some groceries and go to work. At the USO dances there is always a crowd of soldiers and cadets and an astonishingly adequate supply of girls. Bert F. Gould, who runs the place, seems to have a knack for it.

The orchestra, which plays for both the USO dances and those at the town country club (which accepts military memberships at bargain rates), is supplied by Foster Field. It plays better than most Army orchestras and louder than any. However, this is by no means the first martial music Victoria ever heard.

In the Civil War the Lone Star Rifles of Victoria and the Victoria Blues were the very first to volunteer in Texas, a fact which bespeaks great celerity on their part. Earlier still, Victoria had entertained the New Orleans Grays, the Alabama Red Rovers and old Davy Crockett and his Tennessee Boys as they passed that way in their quest for Santa Anna's ears.

In fact, Victoria once had an intriguing little war all its own, a war directed by Martin de Leon, who founded the town. In a pet with the Indians who persisted in stealing his horses and killing his cattle, Señor de Leon, according to Noah Smithwick, "organized his retainers into an army, and mounting a four-pounder swivel gun on a jackass, set out to annihilate the tribe. He ran them to cover, brought his artillery to bear and touched it off, but he did not take the precaution to brace up the jackass, and the recoil turned him a flying somersault, landing him on top of the gun with his feet in the air. . . . The Mexicans got around him and tried to boost him, but the jackass had had enough of that kind of fun and philosophically declined to rise. . . . By that time the Indians had disappeared."

The only thing (and it is a minor one) that keeps the relations between Victoria and its present military guests from being too perfect to be true is the occasionally unsuppressible desire of the pursuiters to buzz a herd of cattle. This is done by flying low over cowboys and cows, changing propeller pitch, and opening the throttle. Almost invariably the herd stampedes. An hour or two later the rancher, hot and mad from chasing frantic cattle through the thorny brush, phones the post and, having already grown air-wise, gives the type of plane, its number, and the time of attack. Result: the pilot gets a fat wad of demerits.

The sole respect in which the town has fallen down on the Army is its failure to supply an adequate, well-regulated red light district. On May 1, there were only two girls "on the line" in Dutch Lane. The rest were in jail. "I don't know what we're going to do," Miss Daisy, proprietress of one of the principal establishments, says. "I've only got one girl now and the town is getting such a bad name in our profession that the girls are afraid to come here." Asked how she got along with the soldiers, Miss Daisy said, "Just fine. You must remember the Air Corps gets very high type boys."

The sheriff's department thinks the same thing. "We just don't have any trouble with those boys," the sheriff said. "If one or two of them get a little full or have a fight, the M.P.'s pick them up. But most of the time they just behave."

In May word reached Victoria that the Army was going to build a bigger air base on the other side of town. The town was delighted. This time the cowmen in front of the Manhattan Cafe whittled no faster.

3

It is true that Texas makes no cannon. It's also true that most shortstops can't pitch. But a team composed only of pitchers couldn't win ball games any more than a country supplied only with cannon could win wars.

What, then, has huge, agrarian Texas to contribute to America's military strength that the industrial East doesn't have and has to have? How much wealth and power that in a bank statement would be termed "quickly available?"

It's got over eleven billion barrels of oil stored where the biggest bomb ever made can't hurt it. It's got a quarter of a million square miles of land. And land means not only food and minerals with which to win a war—it means people who are more utterly dedicated to winning because they have lived close to that land, because it is meaningful and sacred to them, and because it is theirs. It also means the regenerative quality that makes a nation able to recover from a war.

Too, that much land means room which, coupled with Texas weather, provides good flying conditions, particularly for pilot training. It doesn't matter how many planes you've got if you haven't got the fliers.

As this is written, more man-hours of aviation training are being flown in Texas than in any other comparable section in the universe. It happens that I've just returned from a tour of Texas' air training stations, and they are the most fabulous sight I have ever seen, a spectacular expression of the vitality of this nation.

Again, through an accident of weather and space, the daring people, the tough people, are congregating in Texas. Again, things so bold that they stagger the imagination are happening in Texas.

On my junket, I paused at the Naval Air Training Base in Corpus Christi. As I was flying over its incredible expanse, the pilot, a man in his early thirties, Lieutenant-Commander C. C. McCauley, chatting over his shoulder, said, "They sent four of us fellows down here to plan this base. It started out pretty modestly. Then one day we looked up and discovered we'd spent a hundred million dollars."

Somehow it was the best bargain I ever saw.

"Almost every time we buy an outlying field," he added, "we also have to pay for an oil well or two which happens to be on it."

At the present time, there is one mammoth base field at Corpus, three auxiliary fields of impressive proportions, and twenty outlying fields scattered over the adjacent coastal ranches.

The Naval Base covers, within its precincts, hundreds of square miles and is, as a unit, entirely comprehensive, giving training in every branch of naval aviation. The Army does things differently Perhaps because it's operating in so much larger figures, it has striven for and accomplished decentralization.

The show place of the Army Air Force is at Randolph Field, Texas, some eighteen miles out of San Antonio. Its installations are permanent and beautiful. The turf of its field is covered with wild flowers in the spring. The lawns are lovely, the houses charming. Randolph Field is an efficient training unit, an enormously pleasant symbol.

Wearing its war paint, the Army Air Force is different. Brooks Field (observation) and Kelly Field (advanced training and Classification Center), both also near San Antonio, are ugly, jerry-built places in which young men are carefully taught to kill great numbers of people quickly.

But the point is that each phase of the Army training program has schools devoted entirely to that phase. There are pre-flight schools for receiving, orienting and processing dodos (Air Force rookies). Primary training, basic training, observation, navigation, bombardiering, pursuit piloting, twin-engined piloting, and gunnery are each taught in a separate school. It is the production-line system—since hundreds of thousands of units cannot be produced by handicraft methods. For in this vast program almost everything proceeds with intelligence, energy, and spirit toward astronomical expansion.

The only depressing aspect of the whole program, and perhaps we are fortunate that there is but one example, is the utterly unfelicitous placing of great and important Ellington Field at Houston.

It was supposed to be a bombardment school, but Houston has the same jackass-killing climate as that

of near-by Chambers County which Pat Boyt complained
of earlier in this book. On those days when the ceiling
isn't too low for bombing practice, the humidity, to
put it daintily, is too high.

When it was found that bombardment training here
was wholly impractical, Ellington had to be converted
into a twin-engined pilot school and Replacement
Center. And there it now sits, be-fogged, be-rained, be-
mired, wasting precious hours of precious personnel and
precious bi-motored training planes—it may, one hopes,
give a useful preview of London weather to our fledge-
lings. But the field is immovably there, the endless con-
crete runways planted firmly in the mushy earth (fields
more realistically located are able to operate most effi-
ciently from sod landing areas), and little can be done
about it.

Originally, Houston had set out to get *three* airdromes
but, worse luck to our various enemies, the other two
got away.

Most of Texas' flying fields lie farther west where
the earth is dry, and "the skies," as you very well
know, "are not cloudy all day." And here the many
young Americans who have quit their colleges and their
careers are being trained to do the fastest and most telling
killing, to live close to death and, if this war is to be
won, to win it.

Supplying this pilot training program is the huge
(half a square mile) North American Aircraft factory
in Dallas. The much larger assembly plant for Con-

solidated bombers is at Fort Worth. In the same vicinity aircraft motors are also made.

But so far as actual personnel is concerned, the Air Force establishments in Texas are small compared to the Army camps in which every branch of the service is stationed. And these aren't occupied entirely by strangers. Texas claims more Army enlisted men per capita than any other state, and ten per cent of the entire personnel of the Navy. Of that group of fighting amphibians, the United States Marine Corps, thirty per cent hail from the Alamo state. At least these were the latest available figures when war began.

Besides plenty of room and a warm climate suitable for all kinds of training activities, Texas land also affords enormous quantities of good red meat for the bellies on which armies march. Its uncrowded spaces support six million plus head of cattle to feed the best fed nation and Army and Navy in the world, as well as their allies. This same land yields nearly two million hogs, ten million sheep, which in turn means eighty million pounds of wool each year.

If America wanted an army of toughies, tough as Popeye, the Sailor, and if a diet of spinach would do it, Texas could handle the job, with its production of millions of bushels of spinach a year. At the same time we could send the armies of Chiang Kai-shek sixteen million bushels of rice. And to Marshal Timoshenko's army two hundred million pounds of cabbage. We could send cotton enough to clothe them all.

We have hay and grain for all the cavalry of all the

armies now in the field. For barracks we can supply a billion and a quarter board feet of pine lumber per year with our present facilities. From the waste wood, we'll make a hundred thousand tons of sorely needed newsprint.

But, literally, we have not yet scratched the surface—and beneath the surface our greatest wealth lies.

Available for the manufacture of explosives, are over a million and a half tons of Texas sulphur a year. This is eighty-five per cent of the national output. Hard by these sulphur deposits, magnesium, which is essential to the making of light metal alloys as well as explosives, and which a few years ago cost five dollars a pound, is now extracted from Texas sea water at the rate of 19,000 tons per year and supplied to the government at a few cents per pound.

Lignite coal we have almost without limit and almost at the buyer's own price, say seventy-five cents a ton. In a pinch we could scrape up some eight billion tons of bituminous.

Also this fecund Texas earth yields copper, lead, mercury (300,000 pounds per year), natural limestone, asphalt by the hundreds of thousands of tons, cement into the multiple millions of barrels. And for our naval blimps, there is the world's largest supply of helium, the non-inflammable lifting gas.

Finally, there are vast deposits of iron ore in East Texas, which until the present have not been exploited, but blast furnaces are now to be built in Houston for its conversion into metal. But for a long time, however valuable a contribution Texas may make to this nation's need for metal, that contribution will stand in relative unimportance to the great categories of things vital to warfare that Texas can so abundantly supply: fuel, fiber, food—and men.

To implement that last assertion, it might be well to regard a single incident out of the somewhat breezy and over-all historical sketch already given. Having received an impression of the full picture, let's look at close range at a single, significant detail.

17. The Misadventure of Some Gentlemen Abroad

$\mathcal{T}$HE winter days were clear and bright and sharp. The needling shine of dry white earth, of white adobe walls, punished the eye. Rattlesnakes threaded their way over the white dust. The earth was armed with sharp stones and thorned plants. All around the ancient town of San Antonio de Bexar the land, and the feeling of the land, was the same: brightness, whiteness, fangs and thorns. There was in it no suggestion of comfort or of mercy. At night the coyotes banded together, and when they found a rabbit they drove it in relays until it was spent. Then they seized it and, as it screamed, they tore and devoured it.

Within the flat white town of twenty-five hundred souls there were several churches. It was cool in these churches, and heaven, in the eyes of the people who worshipped there, was a cool place where dawn was followed by twilight and there were soft grass and cool springs and no sharp stones.

One of these churches was called the Alamo. It had been built by the Spaniards and the newly converted Indians, who were brought to understand that industry was a part of godliness. Connected with this church was an enclosed compound, to which the soldiers of the King of Spain might, in extremity, repair. Barracks bisected this compound, and water was ditched in from the river. In all, this structure enclosed some four acres.

The walls of the chapel were four feet thick. While it was being built, the babies of San Antonio had grown sallow and thin, since all the milk that the town produced had gone to enrich the mortar which held the stones together. For not only did these walls need to stand against their enemies, they had to be of a quality pleasing to the Deity. But when the roof was built on the chapel, God had turned His face away and that roof had fallen upon the first celebrants of His mysterious beatitude and crushed them.

A hundred years later, after Mexico had passed from the tyranny of Spain to the tyranny of Santa Anna, there had been two states which stood against his dictatorship: Zacatecas and Texas. Zacatecas now lay crushed, its local troops butchered, its women raped, its towns looted. General Santa Anna had, as was his custom, made his disapproval explicit.

And when, in 1836, word came that Santa Anna was forming a huge force on the Rio Grande with San Antonio as his first objective, Colonel Neill, in command of eighty sick and wounded men at the Alamo, pleaded with the Texas government for supplies and reinforcements. But the government itself was split with dissension over the Matamoros expedition. General Houston, though unable to dissuade the army in general, managed nevertheless to dispatch a small detachment to the Alamo.

"Col. Bowie will leave here in a few hours for Bexar, with a detachment of from 20–50 men," Houston wrote to Governor Smith on January 17. "I have ordered the fortifications in the town of Bexar to be demolished, and if you should think fit, I will remove all the cannon and other munitions of war, . . . blow up the Alamo and abandon the place, as it will be impossible to keep up the station with volunteers. . . . "

Governor Smith would know who Bowie was. That name meant something all over Texas, Louisiana, Arkansas and Mexico.

Jim Bowie now, at forty-one, was a ghost. In the past, he'd made fortunes in sugar cane, bogus land titles, and in slaves which he'd bought wholesale from the pirate Jean Lafitte for a dollar a pound. Also contributing to his renown was a simple and highly effective instrument of destruction.

The bowie knife, a kind of dirk which he'd designed,

had been named for him. But it took his name chiefly because of the way he used it, since with it he'd killed adversaries armed with everything from pistols to sword canes. When his intuition told him that some psychological preparation would render his opponent more easily killed, Bowie would invite him to hold one end of a handkerchief in his teeth while he, Bowie, bit the other end as they fought with these knives. For Bowie was shrewd and wanted terror to fight on his side.

In 1831 he had married the beautiful Ursula Veramendi, daughter of one of Mexico's first families, and become a solid citizen and begun the cultivation of virtues more respectable than those for which he'd previously been celebrated. Then, in the third year of this union, the plague had cut down Ursula Bowie and the two Bowie children, and Jim Bowie had become a ghost, a grinning ghost with nothing left inside him but hurt, whisky, and hell.

Now, according to Houston's instructions, Colonel Bowie was on his way to the Alamo with instructions to abandon the place before a blow was struck.

Meanwhile Governor Smith, though unable to get money or provisions to the Alamo, wrote Lieutenant Colonel William Barret Travis, relieved him of his post as superintendent of recruiting, and ordered him to raise a hundred men and proceed to the threatened fortress.

Barret Travis, tall, twenty-seven years old, had been throughout Texas's pre-war days its most violent advocate of war. He had fired the first shot, led the first attack.

In reply to Smith's order, he wrote:

> Burnam's, Colorado, Jany 29th 1836
>
> To His Excellency Henry Smith, Governor of the State of Texas:
>
> . . . Not having been able to raise 100 volunteers agreeably to your orders, and there being so few regular troops together, I beg that your Excellency will recall the order for me to go to Bexar in command of so few men. I am willing, nay anxious, to go to the defense of Bexar, and I have done everything in my power to equip the enlisted men and get them off. But, Sir, I am unwilling to risk my reputation (which is ever dear to a soldier) by going off into the enemy's country with such little means, so few men, and them so badly equipped—the fact is there is no necessity for my services to command these few men. The company officers will be amply sufficient. . . . Therefore, I hope your Excellency will take my situation into consideration and relieve me from the orders which I have hitherto received. . . . Otherwise I shall feel it due to myself to resign my commission. . . .

Governor Smith did not dignify this presumptuous communication with a reply. That he ignored it was a burning rebuke to the hypersensitive lieutenant colonel with his flair for dramatic posturing, and his highly respectful attitude toward himself. Yet Travis, tired, bitter, and disappointed, having anticipated a far different role as the leader of the Matamoros expedition, a role full of assorted gallantries, of dashing cavalry charges and the like, took his medicine and proceeded to the dismal, static hopelessness of the Alamo.

Another colonel, His Garrulous, Jocular Nibbs, The Honorable David Crockett, who, by the grace of God and the intemperate admiration of the people of Tennessee for good bear hunters, was late of the Congress of the United States, was also making his way to the Alamo.

In Congress the Honorable David had offered a
resolution for the government to sell West Point and
give the proceeds to the less affluent voters. But when
such legislative brilliance failed to gain his re-election
in 1835, he assembled his constituents and told them
that he was going to Texas and that they could go to
hell.

Rigging himself out in a coonskin cap and other
vestments in agreement therewith, he took up his
journey, pausing long enough in Nacogdoches to make
a few speeches, denude the town of fried chicken and
pound cake, and attach to himself a company of sixteen
volunteers. These he captioned Davy Crockett's Tennessee Boys, and, after making a farewell speech on
his own greatness as a legislator, went on to the Alamo.

Jim Bowie and his men got there first. On February
2, he wrote to Governor Smith:

DEAR SIR;
    . . . All I can say of the soldiers stationed here is compli-
mentary to both their courage and their patience. But it is the
truth and your Excellency must know it, that great and just
dissatisfaction is felt here for the want of a little money to pay
the small but necessary expenses of our men. . . . No other man
in the army besides Colonel Neill could have kept men at this
post under the neglect that they have experienced. Both he and
myself have . . . tried . . . to raise funds but . . . it has
been to no purpose.
    Relief at this post in men, money, and provisions is of vital
importance and is wanted instantly. . . . It does seem certain
that an attack is shortly to be made on this place. . . . Colonel
Neill and myself have come to the solemn resolution that we
will rather die in these ditches than give it up to the enemy. . . .

Thus wrote the man who had gone to the Alamo with instructions for its demolition and abandonment.

We would rather die in these ditches. . . .

Bowie had brought thirty men, arriving the nineteenth of January. Travis with twenty-five came on the morning of February 3. The doughty legislator Crockett, with his sixteen Tennessee Boys, got there four days later on February 7.

But hardly had the three parties arrived, when word came that Colonel Neill's family was all sick. There was nothing for him to do but go home and look out for them. Which presented the dangerous question: who, in the absence of Colonel Neill, would command the garrison? Jim Bowie, the lethal ghost? Travis, the glory-hungry terrier? Or that exterminator of bears, Indians, and logic: David Crockett?

At once, February 12, Travis sent out a confidential letter to Governor Smith inferring that a full commandancy of the garrison would not be unacceptable to himself.

Neill, conservative, a man of family, favored the abysmally sober and serious lieutenant colonel as his successor. He liked Bowie but Bowie was impulsive, dangerous, reckless. Besides, who could promise that when the hour of great decision came, Bowie would be sober enough to recognize it?

Crockett, the great man from Tennessee, did not even compete for the command. He realized it would be difficult to get, and a nuisance if he did.

The first sign of the struggle between Bowie and Travis for the command was stated in a carping letter which Travis wrote Governor Smith on February 13:

> . . . My situation is truly awkward and delicate. Colonel Neill left me in command, but wishing to give satisfaction to the volunteers here [Travis was a Regular] and not wishing to assume any command over them, I issued an order for the election of an officer to command them with the exception of one company of volunteers that had previously engaged to serve under me. Bowie was elected by two small companies, and since his election has been roaring drunk all the time, has assumed all command & is proceeding in a most disorderly and irregular manner—interfering with private property, releasing prisoners sentenced by court martial & by the civil court & turning everything topsy turvy. If I didn't feel my honor and that of my country comprometted, I would leave here instantly for some other point with the troops under my immediate command as I am unwilling to be responsible for the drunken irregularities of any man. . . .

That was Travis's side of the story.

The election he spoke of ordering had been forced on him by the men. Actually when Colonel Neill had tried to turn over the command of the garrison to Travis, the men had seized Colonel Neill and held him in a chair until he had officiated at the elections, where the votes of all the volunteers, to whom the airs of regular officers were always obnoxious, and those of Travis particularly so, went to Bowie.

Thus, with Travis in command of the Regulars, and with Bowie in command of the Volunteers, and with each aspiring to total command, confusion was complete.

Bowie did not write any letters, or have any written, as Travis had had his cohorts do. He stayed drunk because his insides were disintegrating, and went right on releasing prisoners, preferably Mexican. If there were any way to secure the fragile loyalty of the Mexican population of San Antonio, Bowie meant to do it.

And while Bowie's command of the volunteers was haphazard, that of Travis was almost wholly theoretical. He nagged them, never made jokes, and they had seen him beaten in his attempt to exclude Bowie from command. Nobody had ever seen Jim Bowie beaten.

For that matter, the whole question of command was chiefly rhetorical. Each man commanded himself, though he might be persuaded by an officer for whom he had respect. There was not even a regular commissariat at Bexar. The men scattered over the city in squads, getting food where they could, and sleeping when and where they chose.

Most of the volunteers were young men from the East, many of whom had never touched a rifle till they came to Texas. Their average age was twenty-two or three. And most of them had come because they had nothing to lose but their lives. The exact time of their departure from home had, in most cases, been set by a misunderstanding with some girl. A few, of course, were thieves and swindlers. But most of them were young men with momentarily broken hearts who had come to Texas to lose themselves in strange geography and danger—and for a sweepstakes ticket on the riches in the Halls of the Montezumas.

But the February nights to a lone soldier lying upon the earth or a hard floor, or a buffalo or deer hide if he were lucky, were empty with loneliness and haunted by the memory of women. Many of the women were entire and special. Ursula Bowie was one of these. Many were simply anonymous white torsos with marble breasts, smooth stomachs, white thighs. And the men rolled upon their hard beds in virile, tortured loneliness.

What worried the men least of all was the cannon of the enemy. In spite of all reports to the contrary, they thought the Matamoros expedition would deflect the enemy in that direction. But chiefly, they were indifferent. If the enemy came, all right; if he didn't, all right. What they were much more interested in was getting a little pay so they might have the price of a one-shirt laundry bill, of an unstolen, unconfiscated bottle of tequila, of the consolation of a Mexican girl who, placated by a silver coin, had not just hit them with a rock.

Reports that the enemy was approaching in numbers forty or fifty times that of the garrison continued to arrive. But these were brought mostly by mere Mexican travelers, whom Travis and the other Mexican-despisers refused to believe.

Yet the reports were true. Santa Anna's army of 6,000 men was on the march. And its objective was Bexar and the Alamo. General Filísola, Santa Anna's second in command, had urged by-passing this strong point and sweeping over the remainder of Texas, thereby isolating

Bexar and rendering it both useless and untenable to
the Texans. Besides, if the armies operated nearer to the
coast, supplies from Mexico could be brought by sea.
That was not Santa Anna's way. He wanted none of
the enemy in his rear. Whatever resistance might be
encountered he meant to crush. All those he found bearing arms against him he meant not only to capture but
to exterminate. At noon on February 23, the Mexican
army reached the heights north of the Alazan. They had
arrived at Bexar.

Meanwhile in San Antonio, though the Texans
had refused to believe that Santa Anna's armies were
approaching, the Mexican population had begun a
quiet, general evacuation of the town. Excitement
among them was intense and silent. If a family, piled
on top of a cart containing all its possessions, were
asked where it was going, the father replied casually
that after a great deal of thought he'd decided to go
to the country and farm. In this way the truth, the
desperate reality of the situation, approached the
Texans from behind and laid a cold hand on their
shoulders.

A sentry was posted in the bell tower of San Fernando
church and told to keep his eyes glued to the west.
Near noon on the twenty-third he sighted moving
figures, the glitter of lances, and began ringing the
church bell. However, the figures suddenly disappeared,
and the crowd that gathered was furious and freely
voiced its view of the kind of idiot that gave such false
alarms for a joke.

But Travis, who had previously maintained no spy service (the horses were kept in a pasture five miles away and nobody wanted to walk out there after them), called for volunteer scouts to ride out and reconnoiter.

Dr. John Sutherland and John W. Smith, both having horses in town, offered to go. After agreeing that the sentry on top of the church should give the alarm if he saw them returning at a run, they set out on the Laredo road, which was still muddy from that morning's rain. Upon reaching the crest of a hill about a mile and a half out of town, the two scouts saw the Mexican cavalry, formed in battle line, the commander riding up and down in front of it, waving his sword, and apparently giving orders. Pausing only long enough to estimate the forces before them at from twelve to fifteen hundred, the scouts wheeled their horses and began racing back to town. During this sprint, Dr. Sutherland's horse slipped in the mud, fell, and seriously injured his rider's knee.

The sentry seeing them, banged away at the church bell. At once Travis assembled his men in the Main Plaza, then marched them across the river to the fortress of the Alamo.

Now the returning scouts found the men marvelously changed, working ferociously, and eager for orders. Most of them were planting cannons, bracing doors, and loading guns. As Sutherland and Smith rode into the enclosure, they met Crockett, who went with them to Travis. Sutherland, too crippled to dismount, gave his report from his horse.

Travis asked if he could stand a ride to Gonzales. Sutherland said he'd try, and Smith volunteered to go with him.

"And here I am, Colonel," Crockett said. "Assign me to some place, and me and my Tennessee boys will defend it."

Travis looked at him, smiled, was glad he was there, and told him to defend the picket wall on the south side from the barracks to the church. Then Travis wrote a hasty note:

> Commandancy of Bexar,
> Feb. 23rd. 3o'clock P.M., 1836
> To Andrew Ponton, Judge, and Citizens of Gonzales:
> The enemy in large force is in sight. We want men and provisions. Send them to us. We have 150 men and are determined to defend the Alamo to the last. Give us assistance.
> W. B. TRAVIS—COL. COMMANDING
> P. S. Send an express to San Felipe with news night and day.
> TRAVIS.

This he gave to his couriers, who, taking an indirect course, headed out around the town which was already in the hands of the Mexicans who were establishing their batteries. By now Santa Anna had had a red flag raised over the tower of San Fernando church. It signified: no quarter.

Immediately Travis ordered it to be answered by a shot from the eighteen pounder, but as the shot was fired, the Mexicans sounded a parley and ran up a white flag. Now without consulting Travis, Bowie sent out a flag of truce and a note. If they wanted to talk, why not talk to them? Postponement was on the Texas side.

His note said:

Commander of the Army of Texas:

   Because a shot was fired from a cannon of this fort at the time
that a red flag was raised over the tower, and because a little
afterward they told me that a part of your army had sounded a
parley, which, however, was not heard before the firing of the
said shot, I wish, Sir, to ascertain if it be true that a parley was
called, for which reason I send my second aid, Benito Jameson,
under guarantee of a white flag which I believe will be respected
by you and your forces. God and Texas!
Fortress of the Alamo, February 23, 1836

JAMES BOWIE
(Rubric)

Commander of the volunteers of Bexar to the Commander of the
invading forces below Bejar.

It was gone before Travis knew what was afoot. And
he was furious. Damn Jim Bowie's interfering soul to
hell. To parley now could only signify weakness on
the part of the garrison. Besides, what could such
negotiations offer the Texans other than unconditional
surrender, which, it went without saying, was unacceptable? There was nothing to do but fight. A fight
which the Texans hadn't a hundred-to-one chance to
win. And since the only thing left was certain death,
why not do it with dignity? Why not do it fighting
instead of talking? Travis's life was important to him.
He didn't want to die. But if he had to, the *way* in which
he died was of great concern to him. It must be an inspira-
tion to all Texans. It must be dramatic and ennobling.
That being the case, he didn't want any half-drunk
incompetent degrading his last hour with any snivelling
appeals for mercy.

Soon Ben Jameson was back with the reply:

> As the aid-de-Camp of his Excellency, the President of the
> Republic, I reply to you, according to the order of his Excel-
> lency, that the Mexican army cannot come to terms under any
> conditions with rebellious foreigners to whom there is no other
> recourse left, if they wish to save their lives, than to place them-
> selves immediately at the disposal of the Supreme Government
> from whom alone they may expect clemency after some con-
> siderations [are taken up]. God and Liberty!
>
> JOSÉ BATRES to JAMES BOWIE
>
> This is a copy. JOSÉ BATRES
>   (Rubric)
> General Headquarters of San Antonio de Bejar
> Feb. 23, 1836

The fight was irrevocably on.

Inside the fortress the bad blood between Travis and
Bowie had again come to the surface. Yet on the very
next morning, February 24, Bowie came down with
what was diagnosed as typhoid-pneumonia. Exposure,
alcohol, and exhaustion had joined in inviting it.
Besides, while situating some artillery a few days before,
he'd got a nasty fall off one of the walls. Now even
the ghost of Bowie was disintegrating.

And Travis was glad to have this trouble-maker,
this competitor for the affection of the men, out of the
way. At last he knew where he stood. Command,
absolute and utter, was clenched in his own hands. Now
he knew what the orders would be. He looked at his
ragged men. They were all his and, whether they liked
him or not, they were tough and brave. His rival,
the last appeaser, the last pepper-gut lover, was out

of the conflict. The situation was coherent. He was dealing in certainties. The possibilities had been reduced to two: win or die.

He went to his room and wrote a letter. Now that the pressure was on, Travis's pretensions either fell aside or fittingly into place. In the burning heat of high determination, knowing that the eye of history was upon him and that his great hour had come, he took up a quill pen and wrote:

Commandancy of the Alamo,
Bexar, Feby. 24th, 1836

To the People of Texas and All Americans in the world—

FELLOW CITIZENS AND COMPATRIOTS: I am besieged with a thousand or more of the Mexicans under Santa Anna. I have sustained a continual Bombardment and cannonade for 24 hours and have not lost a man. The enemy has demanded a surrender at discretion, otherwise, the garrison are to be put to the sword, if the fort is taken. I have answered the demand with a cannon shot, and our flag still waves proudly from the walls. *I shall never surrender or retreat.* Then, I call upon you in the name of Liberty, of patriotism, and every thing dear to the American character, to come to our aid with all dispatch. The enemy is receiving reinforcements daily and will no doubt increase to three or four thousand in four or five days. If this call is neglected, I am determined to sustain myself as long as possible and die like a soldier who never forgets what is due his own honor and that of his country. VICTORY or DEATH.

WILLIAM BARRET TRAVIS
Lt. Col. Comdt.

P. S.

The Lord is on our side. When the enemy appeared in sight we had not three bushels of corn. We have since found in deserted houses 80 to 90 bushels and got into the walls 20 or 30 head of Beeves.

TRAVIS

On the day before Travis had written this letter, Jim Bonham, an old school friend of his from Alabama, had met his couriers to Gonzales. Bonham was coming from Goliad where he'd been sent by Travis two weeks earlier to urge Fannin to bring his force of 420 men to reinforce the Alamo. Now Sutherland and Smith told Bonham that the Alamo was surrounded and that it would be suicide for him to go there. He was not convinced. Two hours later, having successfully crossed the enemy's lines, he reported to Travis.

"Are they coming?" Travis asked.

Bonham said he thought so, that you could never be sure of a force of volunteers, but that he was pretty sure they were coming.

Travis walked back and forth a few times, tense and hoping. With Fannin's force from Goliad he'd have near 600 men. With that many, and perhaps a hundred from Gonzales, he'd command 700 men. If each had five loaded rifles, that would make 3,500 guns. And with that many he'd pour so much fire on Santa Anna's attacking columns that they'd buckle and break and run over themselves getting away.

What of provisions for so many men? As long as they were drawing blood from the enemy, as long as these old walls stood, they could live off the fire in their own guts, on old harness, their own dung, anything.

The walls must be made to stand. He ordered the men to begin throwing dirt against the bases so that despite the increasing cannonade at least the lower part of the walls would stand. But in case that too should be blasted out of the earth, he had trenches dug inside.

The work went on all night and when morning came, fires were built, a beef killed, and the quarters started turning on a spit. The tired men shaved off slivers of the succulent, browning exterior while the remainder went on turning and cooking.

All day the cannonade continued and grew. It was not good to stand against the ancient walls for fear they crumble and tons of stone fall upon you. Yet it was less good to move in the open compound where a cannon ball might suddenly divide you into halves.

In the afternoon, Travis called for volunteers. The fortress was almost devoid of firewood. Worse, on the south side of the fortress there was a row of Mexican huts, called *jacals*, that might give cover to a column forming to storm the walls. He wanted as much wood torn from them and corn taken out of them as possible. The rest he wanted burnt.

The number of volunteers was an embarrassment to Travis, and he had to reduce it in order that the fort not be emptied. The men weren't doing this for Travis. It needed doing.

After midnight then, the raiding party dropped softly over the walls on moccasined feet. A small protecting force carried rifles, the rest, only their knives. Quietly now they moved upon the huts, all of them realizing the great desirability of silently, deftly cutting a Mexican sentry's throat rather than shooting him, which would reveal both their presence and position.

When the huts were reached, those who were to carry firewood gathered up what wooden objects lay loose, and sawed in two the rawhide thongs which held the boards in place. When these men were loaded and their retreat well begun, the others fired the interiors of the huts so that for a moment or two their own retreat would not be lighted, and then ran at top speed back to the fortress, softly calling the password as they neared it. Soon all hands were safely inside, and the night was coming aglow with the fire from the burning *jacals*.

But hardly had the dawn begun to break when the sentries at the wall saw a battalion forming in the direction of the main gate, and cried out the alarm. Soon they saw the Mexicans were trying to plant a battery to bear on the gate, and the Texans opened up with everything they had that would shoot in that direction. And though the Mexicans were being supported by other batteries already planted, the blistering profusion of Texas grape and canister and musket balls drove them back.

Eight Mexicans had been struck. Two had said their last *Ave Maria*. Two Mexican camp followers, who'd followed these men 500 miles on foot to cook for them, to be near them, sat through the remainder of the bright day staring upon this strange and empty and brutal land.

But with the coming of night, the Mexicans, covered by some old houses the Texans had neglected to destroy, established a battery 300 yards south of the Alamo gate, and another 1,000 yards to the southeast. Also, in case the Texans should attempt to escape, or in case reinforcements might try to reach them, General Andrade's cavalry was posted on the Gonzales road.

Not an hour after the first Mexican battery had been established before the gate, the night-roving Texans discovered it and fired the straw and wooden houses that protected it. And a strong, biting north wind which had blown up near nine o'clock spread the fire to still other buildings.

As the night began to fade, a few of the Texans who were sacking a neighborhood near the fortress were found by a detachment of Mexican cavalry.

"Don't run!" the leader yelled. "They'll chop you down with their cutlasses. Fire steady and fall back. Steady. Keep your eyes on 'em."

Coolly, firing with deadly effect, the Texans retreated until they came within the covering fire of the fortress, then thankfully, with immense relief, they turned and ran. And when a check was made of the returning party, every man was there.

Meanwhile the bombardment of the fort, the arrival of Santa Anna's reinforcements, continued.

Travis wrote an account to Houston of the preceding day's contest over the planting of the cannon at the gate, in which he pointed out that the Sage of Tennessee, "The Honorable David Crockett, was seen at all points, animating the men to do their duty. Our numbers are few and the enemy still continues to approximate his works to ours. I have every reason to apprehend an attack from his whole force very soon. . . . Do hasten on aid to me as rapidly as possible, as from the superior number of the enemy, it will be impossible to keep them out much longer. . . . "

He might have added: "It's cold here now. My men have no blankets. No one comes to stand beside us, to die with us. We are feeling a loneliness, a sadness beyond expression. Only the fire within ourselves warms and keeps us going. It is a good fire, but we've lived on it alone now for so very long."

Later in the day the enemy tried to cut the fortress water supply. It failed and a few more Mexicans, the best, the most daring, the quickest volunteers, were sent to hell by Texas bullets.

Then it was night again and the Texans burnt more houses around newly planted artillery of the enemy, completely denuded of cover the land across which the Mexicans would have to attack.

That night, the night of February 27, Travis had been unable to sleep. Near daylight, in desperation for action and the sight of a human face in the room he was coming to hate more than all the rooms he'd ever known, he sent for his old friend Bonham. Travis thought, "I can count on Jim Bonham. As long as he's breathing, he's doing his job. And he'll keep on breathing because he's got the kind of guts that make luck."

Travis loved Bonham. In Travis's scheme of things Bonham was almost his equal. Bonham would try anything, and there would be a strangely swift, breath-taking, and unnerving quality of lightning in his trying.

Bonham came in shaking off sleep. Travis was walking the floor thinking.

"Ride to Goliad, Jim," he said. "And make Fannin bring them on. Tell him anything, promise him anything. I know why he doesn't come. Because I'm in command here. Tell him he can keep his command over those miserable troops of his if he'll just bring 'em and fight 'em. Offer him joint command with me. Make that clear, Jim. Fire him up some way. Show him that here is where we win or lose. Tell him how thick these walls are and how easy it'd be to shoot a Mexican off the top. Tell him the walls are four feet thick and that they are our skin. Tell him what smooth ground the Mexicans have to cross to get here. Tell him it'll be like shooting fish in a water barrel. But also tell him how simple it'll be to get his men here after dark. Tell him our boys wander all over hell once the sun goes down. Go get 'im, Jim."

Bonham left without saying anything at all.

And to Travis that was soothing and wonderful, because when Jim Bonham got quiet, just terribly quiet, that was when he got good.

Travis slept a few hours, awakened occasionally by the now desultory bombardment.

All that day and the next and the next the cannonade continued; the batteries were inched closer and closer. Travis sent out two more couriers to try to speed reinforcements. Grim despair was settling over the Alamo. No longer were the men haunted by the thought of the flashing thighs of white women. All they wanted now was sleep and whisky and the sight of one of their fellows running across the compound yelling, "They've come! The men from Goliad are here!"

And the sadness, the cold yet fighting despair of the men at the gun ports, the knowledge that they were trapped and would soon feel the crashing agony of bayonets in their bellies, all this stark hopelessness, was but rosin to the flashing bow of the Congressman from Tennessee. As he saw the lines of misery cut into the faces of the men, he would strike up a jig and sashay in semicircles about his doomed fellows. Making up little songs containing their own names, songs of poor dunces who had to stand by a wall like naughty children to keep out the magnificent marksmen of Santa Anna, whose guns were fashioned to such length that they might not shoot off certain important and intimate portions of their own anatomy. For if that happened, who would cook for the Mexican army when all of the camp followers went home?

Lewd and brave and jocular, most of his songs were, especially the ones about the heroic and comical love life of "His Ex Cellenc ySan ta Annnna." Or he'd sing a popular song of the moment, "Will You Come to My Bower I Have Shaded for You," with a suitably licentious set of extra lyrics for His Excellency.

Or perhaps he would sing fabulous tales of his own prowess as a bear hunter, a lover, or as a Jovian defender of the people's rights. And though the men might not have felt like laughing, there was not much else they could do, because he'd keep on clowning and cutting monkeyshines until they did.

Yet the sight of the continual arrival of soldiers into the Mexican camp was not one easily fiddled away, and when old Davy had fiddled himself out, the men soon grew brittle again with strain and resentfulness and were apt to grow surly to their officers and refuse to execute minor orders. Bowie, who had grown ghost-thin, would have his bed brought outside for a quarter hour to talk to the men, to remind them that Colonel Travis was in command, and that any of the volunteers who refused to obey Travis, and that damn quick, would have to answer to himself. To do otherwise than to obey smartly, he pointed out, would only hasten their impending reunion in hell.

On one of these times he asked Travis if the ammunition could be spared for taking a couple of cannon shots at a very official looking building in the Mexican camp, one which officers were continually entering and leaving. The ammunition could not be spared, but Travis consented.

And though the second shot plowed into this house, which actually was Santa Anna's headquarters, and burst it open, His Excellency was elsewhere, bent upon more tender pursuits. A few days earlier he had encountered a Mexican girl of startling freshness and beauty, and the generalissimo, weary of his professional exertions, had honored and was at the time still honoring this girl of humble birth with attentions of the most intimate character, a circumstance that was just now more than any other retarding the investment of the Alamo.

The chill night of March 1 fell upon the tired men of the Alamo. Those that slept, slept huddled by their loaded guns at the walls. Santa Anna had them groggy with strain and suspense.

Then the guards at the gate heard the password given. They recognized the voice of the courier, John W. Smith. In a matter of seconds the word flashed over the fortress that Smith had come back, bringing with him thirty-two men from Gonzales, raising the strength of the garrison to approximately 180 men.

And though it was a custom at the fort for newcomers to roast the meat and make the cornbread for the rest of the garrison at their first meal, that tradition went into abeyance this night. With inexpressible emotions, the veterans of the siege cooked the supper.

"Now," Travis thought, "our luck's turned. Surely Fannin will be on later tonight or tomorrow night. Then, fighting like fiends, rising above ourselves, we'll beat off Santa Anna's thousands. We'll hold these old walls. We'll live."

Yet when morning came, Fannin's men had not arrived, nor by the morning following. At eleven o'clock on that same morning, the tenth day of the siege, one of the men on the walls yelled, "Open the gates."

He'd seen Bonham burst into the Mexican camp at full speed on his cream-white horse, a white handkerchief, the pre-arranged signal, flying from his hat. He was bent low on the horse's neck, batting it with a mesquite switch and yelling at the top of his lungs. The shock threw the Mexicans momentarily off stride. By the time they'd begun their hurried shooting, Bonham had almost reached the fort. A few seconds later he was inside, unscathed.

And Travis was coming to meet him, walking slowly, with dignity, his guts screwed into a knot of hoping, his face composed, for the benefit of the men.

"Well, Jim?"

"They're not coming, Colonel."

"Thank you, Jim. That was a good ride."

"They . . . they started, then turned back."

"I see."

Colonel Travis walked back to his quarters alone.

There he wrote a letter to the government explaining his situation. He wrote another letter to a friend. It contained several sentences. The important one, the whole reason for the letter being written, was: "Take care of my little boy."

That night he called a meeting of the men and said, "I would be failing in my duty as your commander if I did not point out to you that our situation is without all hope—except in the rare sense that a few determined men may sometimes fuse the fire of their spirits, the strength of their arms and bodies, into a force that is indomitable.

"Many of you are husbands; many, as I am, are fathers. I do not therefore propose to hold you here against your will. For those of you who care to try it, escape is still thoroughly possible. Our couriers have passed through the Mexican lines with impunity. If you're careful, you can get through too.

"I think, however, I should tell you that the Mexicans will never enter this fortress without encountering resistance. I have decided that whatever your various decisions may be, I shall remain.

"Now, to simplify matters, I shall draw a line in the earth with my sword. I will ask those who wish to stay with me, if any should, to cross this line. Those not wishing to make that commitment are free to leave at once."

For a moment the men stood still, looking upon the utterly dedicated figure of their commander. About him there was a kind of peace, a kind of calm, they'd never seen there before. The strain of trying to conquer the impossible was no longer there. For the first time Travis was resigned to settle for his best, even if his best wasn't enough. But not only were the men acted upon by this new quality in their commander, their ability, for the very first time, to like him. They were also feeling with a kind of mystical conviction that they themselves belonged here, that here and here only could their full destiny, whatever that might be, be realized. Like the Mexicans who brought the milk their babies needed, brought it without stint or misgiving, and poured it into these walls, the men knew that if they remained here, they remained with God. Whether He chose to protect them was something else. If they left, they left without Him, and without the finest part of themselves.

Besides, it was easy to stand with their somehow reborn commander, who could face certain doom with serenity. After a life of straining to imitate his dream, Travis had now become that dream and was beautiful and inspiring—and certain.

The silence was broken by Bowie.

"Some of you boys set my bed across that line," he said.

And those that carried it across remained across, and the others followed, all but one.

When in the past the men had made jokes with this man, he'd drawn his knife and snarled. But now, though he'd never felt what the others felt, he did feel the sense of defilement that he gave them. He knew he was in the midst of a great, almost religious experience and that he was befouling it.

He sank to the ground and sat on his feet and trembled. But he belonged on a certain side of the line and he remained there.

Soon then, the men boosted him over the wall so that he could run away, and they felt cleansed and ready to fight.

By ten o'clock of the evening of March 5, the Mexican bombardment ceased entirely for the first time in twelve days, and the exhausted Texans fell asleep at the walls. The last remnants of Santa Anna's army had arrived the day before. The Alamo was now surrounded by 5,000 men.

Santa Anna had issued his orders. The infantry was to form in four columns under his ablest officers, with alternate officers appointed in case of need. Each column was supplied with axes, crowbars, and scaling ladders. The light companies of all battalions were merged with the battalion of engineers to form the reserve, which was to be commanded by the Generalissimo. The cavalry, under General Sesma, was placed in the rear to prevent desertion or, should any Texans break out of the fortress, for pursuit. All orders were to be executed in complete silence, with equipment muffled, and all fires extinguished.

Just before dawn the next morning, the lone Alamo sentry, who of all the garrison was not asleep, heard a peculiar sound, vast and soft. Then his blood froze as he realized it was thousands of bare Mexican feet running across the soft dust on all sides, that they were converging upon the fortress. The sentry yelled.

Above the muffled roar of bare feet running, the waking Texans heard a Mexican band in the distant dark strike up the bloodcurdling *Deguello*—the old air by which the Spaniards for centuries had slaughtered their enemies, the air which meant no quarter.

Now the Texans were leaping to their posts and, when they got there, firing at any motion they could sense in the teeming darkness. Travis, running faster than the rest, had reached his crucial post first and manned the cannon at the only broken place in the wall where Mexicans could run through. Crockett's boys were at the south wall firing and loading. The artillery was blasting the columns with canister and grape. But the Mexican tide was in motion. The officers, the surge of the men running in the rear, drove the column over the front ranks as they fell.

Swerving to avoid the blazing fire of the cannon, the columns on the north, south and east, were driven into union, and then, a mighty flood, they gushed up to and over the wall, the living climbing over the dying. As they dropped inside the walls, some were killed before they struck the ground, others had their brains bashed out by Texans clubbing with empty guns, or their heads chopped half off with hunting knives. The rest knelt and fired.

Already Travis, with a hole through his head, was dead at his gun. And Mexicans were running in through the breach in the walls. The Texans, fighting foot by foot, were retreating toward the barracks inside the compound, some falling, the rest fighting with steady fury.

The bull voice of old Davy Crockett was rising above the melee. He was in command now, by natural right, moving too fast to make a good target, bashing skulls, breaking backs, clubbing and dodging. Then a bullet caught Davy in the back and he sat down, and a second later the bayonets shot into him, three of them, and that was all.

The Alamo was without a commander. Bowie, with a bed full of pistols, just killed Mexicans personally until his guns were empty. Then they rushed him, caught him with their bayonets, and tossed him like farmers pitching hay.

Now the Mexicans had forced their way into the

barracks and were killing the men there, giving them the steel in ecstasy and horror—driving the bayonets hard because they were blunt and because human bone and muscle is tough. The feet of running men slid uncontrollably on the slick, sticky earth.

Major Bob Evans saw all the rest of the garrison was dead and he darted through the Mexicans toward the powder magazine, which it had been agreed the last man was to blow. He reached it, struck a fire, thought of the women, Mrs. Dickerson and one or two Mexican women, there for protection, and then, having paused only a fraction of a second, decided to blow the fort anyway, but a slug hit him in the head and he was dead before he could touch off the powder.

Dead now and broken were all the men, and nothing yielded.

The bonny, lovelorn lads from Virginia, Louisiana, Tennessee.

The thirty-two from Gonzales.

Jim Bowie.

Davy Crockett.

Jim Bonham.

Barret Travis.

A pyre was built for their bodies. A hot fire, tall and crackling, a fire that laid smoke upon the Alamo, that passed into the Texas air, consumed them.

The Alamo had fallen.

In Lieu of a Bibliography

Most of the anecdotes Texas knows about itself it learned from Frank Dobie, who has devoted years to uncovering and assembling them. And while most of them are in the common domain, they are still somehow, by moral right, his.

The same is true of Dr. Amelia Williams. Her thesis, *The Siege and Fall of the Alamo*, while being undisputably the standard and most exhaustive work on the subject, is not copyrighted, but few works have been more extensively borrowed from or respected.

But at least a writer knows *when* he is borrowing from Dr. Williams. Dobie's work is so interwoven into the whole literature and life of the Southwest that a good story from whatever source is apt to have been originally set down into print by him.

One of the most rewarding works that bears on the Texas Revolution is Dr. Carlos E. Castañeda's *The Mexican Side of the Texan Revolution*. The picture it gives is a lively one of all the Mexican generals and politicos blaming each other for Mexico's defeat, and spilling significant dirt. None of these hearties, it goes without saying, was any more glib in his own defense than Santa Anna. Dr. Castañeda's book pictures a scene but little unlike the conditions which prevailed in Vichy after the French capitulation to Germany in 1940.

The best source I found on Stephen Austin was Dr. Eugene Barker's scholarly and definitive biography, but no less worthy were the papers of Austin himself, collected and edited by Dr. Barker. They were extremely enlightening and somehow entertaining.

But the most toothsome single volume bearing on the early Texas scene was Marquis James's lively, scholarly, beautifully written and edited, in fact in every way superlatively excellent, biography of Sam Houston, *The Raven*.

The most highly concentrated reservoir of reliable fact concerning Texas is the *Texas Almanac* published by the Dallas *News*.

The various available biographies of Santa Anna I found not much to my taste, but there is a delightful one of Jean Lafitte, subtitled *Gentleman Smuggler*, and written by Mitchell V. Charnley.

I should like to thank the Steck Publishing Company of Austin, Texas, for permission to quote from and draw upon, actually to condense, Noah Smithwick's *The Evolution of a State* or *Recollections of Old Texas Days*.

Incidentally, the report of the Texas Senate, sitting as a High Court of Impeachment at the trial of Governor Jim Ferguson, is anything but dull reading.

I sought information on the Rangers in Walter Prescott Webb's *The Texas Rangers*. I found Sam Bass's story told in Wayne Gard's *Sam Bass*.

For Dallas *News* background I consulted Sam Acheson's 35,000 *Days in Texas*, which is both history and biography of that great journal.

Finally, there are two splendid magazine pieces that have been of much help to me. Both of them appeared in *Fortune*, one on the King Ranch in the December, 1933, issue, the other on Texas generally, in the December, 1939, issue. Both were comprehensive, yet concise.

Most of the Bowie books are vague and legendary, books in which the subject always gets the benefit of the doubt.

Aside from these major sources, I have read some two or three wagonloads of assorted uninteresting source books on Texas, the names of which will profit no one. The majority of them were dusty, at least semi-privately printed little tomes, of interest only to the most serious and unswervable historians.

The living people from whom I sought information were, as a whole, considerably more interesting than the counsel I received from books. Particularly so were the politicos: Jim Ferguson, Jimmy Allred, Harry Crozier, and Coke Stevenson. Paul McClure of Devers told me and showed me everything about the Texas rice industry; his boss, Pat Boyt, about East Texas ranching. Jack Lewis of Rockdale supplied me with an inexhaustible quantity of the lore of oil-field chicanery, Henry Hardin of Socony-Vacuum with the refinery picture. John Newton, vice-president of Socony-Vacuum and director of its Beaumont refinery, helped me obtain a view of Texas oil and refining in relation to the demands of the second World War. Allan and Donna Bartlett, of the Houston *Press*, helped me interpret the Houston scene. Holland McCombs, Time, Inc.'s bureau

286 Texas: *A World in Itself*

man for Texas, suggested many aspects of the general subject that might not otherwise have come to my attention. Bill Owens of A. and M. College knows all about Texas folk music and played for me a substantial part of the six hundred recordings he has made. Dr. Castañeda, in charge of the Texas collection at the University of Texas library, gave me much personal assistance and advice. Dr. Amelia Williams told me many collateral details concerning the Alamo; however, she is not to be blamed for my interpretation of them. My late uncle, Harry Gordon Perry, a raconteur of much zest and talent, has supplied me over the years with many fine Texas anecdotes. Some have been used here. The best ones had to be excluded out of respect for the demands of propriety. A hitchhiker I picked up between Beaumont and Galveston, who was a sometime commercial fisherman, enlightened me copiously on that subject. Of less specialized assistance were Jean T. Hulburd, Dorothy Cameron Disney, and Milton Angus MacKaye. Mr. George P. Isbell, Florence and Frank Rosengren, of San Antonio, gave helpful advice on the manuscript. Finally, Naomi Burton, of Curtis Brown, Ltd., probably garnered for me the most pertinent information of all.

In the actual preparation and editing of this book, my talented and long-suffering wife has performed most of the drudgery connected therewith. Her assistance has been of immeasurable value.

To all these friends and advisers, and particularly to my wife, my profound thanks.

Index